Collins

Integrated Science 2

for the **Caribbean**

T0340408

Gene Samuel & Derek McMonagle

Advisors:

**Shameem Narine, Nadine Victor-Ayers,
Ishaq Mohammed, Sheldon Rivas & Doltan Ramsubeik**

updated

Collins

HarperCollins*Publishers* Ltd
The News Building
1 London Bridge Street
London SE1 9GF

HarperCollins*Publishers*
Macken House, 39/40 Mayor Street Upper,
Dublin 1, DO1 C9W8, Ireland

Updated edition 2017

10 9 8

This book is produced from independently certified FSC™ paper
to ensure responsible forest management.

For more information visit: www.harpercollins.co.uk/green

ISBN 978-0-00-826303-4

Collins® is a registered trademark of HarperCollins*Publishers* Limited

www.collins.co.uk/caribbeanschools

A catalogue record for this book is available from the British Library.

Typeset by QBS Learning
Printed in Great Britain by Martins the Printers

Authors: Gene Samuel & Derek McMonagle
Advisors: Shameem Narine, Nadine Victor-Ayers, Ishaq Mohammed, Sheldon Rivas & Doltan Ramsubeik
Illustrators: QBS Learning
Publisher: Elaine Higgleton
Commissioning Editor: Tom Hardy
Project Management: QBS Learning
Editor: Julianna Dunn
Copy Editor: Niamh O'Carroll
Proofreader: David Hemsley
Cover Design: Gordon MacGilp

Gene Samuel has taught science at Forms 1 and 2 level at St. Joseph's Convent Secondary School, Castries,
St Lucia and is a very experienced science teacher. She has been developing resources for use in her own school
for many years.

Derek McMonagle is a leading writer of science educational materials with world-wide experience. He has
developed courses at primary, secondary and advanced levels for many countries including Jamaica and the UK.

Contents

Introduction – How to use this book

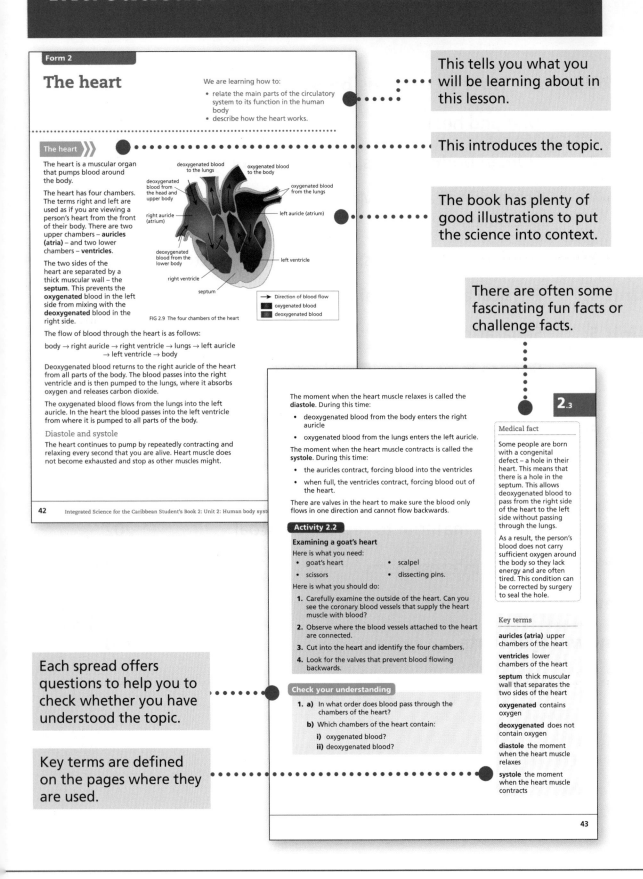

Form 2

The heart

We are learning how to:
- relate the main parts of the circulatory system to its function in the human body
- describe how the heart works.

This tells you what you will be learning about in this lesson.

The heart

The heart is a muscular organ that pumps blood around the body.

The heart has four chambers. The terms right and left are used as if you are viewing a person's heart from the front of their body. There are two upper chambers – **auricles (atria)** – and two lower chambers – **ventricles**.

The two sides of the heart are separated by a thick muscular wall – the **septum**. This prevents the **oxygenated** blood in the left side from mixing with the **deoxygenated** blood in the right side.

The flow of blood through the heart is as follows:

body → right auricle → right ventricle → lungs → left auricle → left ventricle → body

Deoxygenated blood returns to the right auricle of the heart from all parts of the body. The blood passes into the right ventricle and is then pumped to the lungs, where it absorbs oxygen and releases carbon dioxide.

The oxygenated blood flows from the lungs into the left auricle. In the heart the blood passes into the left ventricle from where it is pumped to all parts of the body.

Diastole and systole

The heart continues to pump by repeatedly contracting and relaxing every second that you are alive. Heart muscle does not become exhausted and stop as other muscles might.

deoxygenated blood to the lungs

oxygenated blood to the body

deoxygenated blood from the head and upper body

oxygenated blood from the lungs

right auricle (atrium)

left auricle (atrium)

deoxygenated blood from the lower body

left ventricle

right ventricle

septum

→ Direction of blood flow
■ oxygenated blood
■ deoxygenated blood

FIG 2.9 The four chambers of the heart

This introduces the topic.

The book has plenty of good illustrations to put the science into context.

There are often some fascinating fun facts or challenge facts.

2.3

The moment when the heart muscle relaxes is called the **diastole**. During this time:
- deoxygenated blood from the body enters the right auricle
- oxygenated blood from the lungs enters the left auricle

The moment when the heart muscle contracts is called the **systole**. During this time:
- the auricles contract, forcing blood into the ventricles
- when full, the ventricles contract, forcing blood out of the heart.

There are valves in the heart to make sure the blood only flows in one direction and cannot flow backwards.

Activity 2.2

Examining a goat's heart

Here is what you need:
- goat's heart
- scalpel
- scissors
- dissecting pins.

Here is what you should do:
1. Carefully examine the outside of the heart. Can you see the coronary blood vessels that supply the heart muscle with blood?
2. Observe where the blood vessels attached to the heart are connected.
3. Cut into the heart and identify the four chambers.
4. Look for the valves that prevent blood flowing backwards.

Check your understanding

1. a) In what order does blood pass through the chambers of the heart?
   b) Which chambers of the heart contain:
      i) oxygenated blood?
      ii) deoxygenated blood?

Medical fact

Some people are born with a congenital defect – a hole in their heart. This means that there is a hole in the septum. This allows deoxygenated blood to pass from the right side of the heart to the left side without passing through the lungs.

As a result, the person's blood does not carry sufficient oxygen around the body so they lack energy and are often tired. This condition can be corrected by surgery to seal the hole.

Key terms

auricles (atria) upper chambers of the heart

ventricles lower chambers of the heart

septum thick muscular wall that separates the two sides of the heart

oxygenated contains oxygen

deoxygenated does not contain oxygen

diastole the moment when the heart muscle relaxes

systole the moment when the heart muscle contracts

Each spread offers questions to help you to check whether you have understood the topic.

Key terms are defined on the pages where they are used.

43

Review of Separating mixtures

- A mixture is a physical combination and can therefore be separated using physical means.
- There are various methods of separating a mixture, each based on the physical properties of the components – for example: particle size, volatility and boiling solubility, density.
- The methods of separation that depend on particle size are: filtration, sieving and hand-picking.
- In filtration, a mixture of a solid and a liquid are passed through a filter. The liquid collected is the filtrate and the solid left on the filter is called the residue.
- The methods of separation that depend on volatility and boiling point are: evaporation, distillation and fractional distillation.
- The more volatile a liquid, the lower its boiling point. A very volatile liquid evaporates at room temperature.
- In distillation apparatus, a liquid is boiled off and then its vapour is condensed.
- Simple distillation can be used to separate the solid and liquid components of a solution, or two liquids with very different boiling points.
- Fractional distillation is needed to separate liquids of similar boiling points.
- In a fractionating column, the more volatile liquids are collected further up the column.
- The method of separation that depends on the solubility of the components is chromatography.
- Different inks dissolve at different rates in ethanol, so they travel different distances up the chromatography paper.
- The methods of separation that depend on density are: decanting, use of a separating funnel, centrifugation and sedimentation.

At the end of each group of units, there are pages that list the key topics covered in the units. These will be useful for revision.

At the end of each section, there are special questions to help you and your teacher review your knowledge, see if you can apply this knowledge and check that you can use the science skills that you have developed.

Science, Technology, Education and Mathematics (STEM) activities are included, which present real-life problems to be investigated and resolved using your science and technology skills. These pages are called **Science in practice**.

Review questions on Separating mixtures

1. Match the letter assigned to each description with the number of the method it describes.

	Method		Description
1	centrifugation	a	method by which particle size is separated
2	fractional distillation	b	only the solid is left
3	sieving	c	method used for separation of dyes
4	decanting	d	rotational speed is required
5	evaporation	e	used for separating the parts of a solution
6	sedimentation	f	wine undergoes this separation
7	filtration	g	separation of a mixture of liquids of similar but different boiling points
8	distillation	h	occurs at water treatment plants
9	chromatography	i	natural separation of liquid and insoluble solid that sinks to the bottom

TABLE 5.1

2. You have a mixture of pebbles, sand, salt and iron filings, all in water. Explain how you would separate the mixture into its five different components.

3. a) Describe how fractional distillation works.
   b) Explain how products are obtained from crude oil.

4. Name:
   a) one advantage of distillation compared with evaporation
   b) one disadvantage of distillation compared with evaporation.

5. Explain how separation occurs in the process of chromatography.

6. a) When is a separating funnel used?
   b) Explain how this apparatus works.

7. Draw and label a diagram to show how sedimentation occurs.

8. Describe how centrifugation works.

Investigating pigments in leaves

Plants are green because they contain the pigment chlorophyll. This pigment is essential for the process of photosynthesis. Not all plants have green leaves. Does this mean that they do not contain chlorophyll?

The answer is no, because if the leaves of a plant did not contain chlorophyll they would not be able to make food and therefore would not exist. They do contain chlorophyll but it is masked by other pigments. For example, the presence of pigments called anthocyanins can result in red, blue or purple colouration of leaves.

1. You are going to work in a group of three or four to investigate the pigments present in non-green leaves. The tasks are:
   - to identify local examples of plants that do not have green, or totally green, leaves
   - to devise a method of extracting the colouring matter from leaves
   - to separate the different pigments found in the leaves of a particular plant
   - to separate and then count the number of pigments present.

   a) Look at the leaves of plants found growing locally on open ground, perhaps in gardens or maybe as pot plants.

   What are the names of these plants? Can you find the Latin name as well as the local name?

   Make arrangements to obtain a sample of leaves. If the plants are on open ground, you may just take the leaves. If they are in a garden or on a potted plant, you should ask the permission of the owner. Explain that this won't cause the plants any harm.

   b) How are you going to extract the coloured pigments from the leaf cells? You need to consider:
   - How to crush the plant material. Maybe you could use a mortar and pestle?

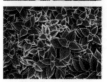

FIG 5.SIP.1 Not all plant leaves are green

Unit 1: Diet and health

Introduction »»

A diet is all of the things that a person eats and drinks.

Food may be placed into groups according to the nutrients it contains. These nutrients are:

- carbohydrates
- fats
- proteins
- vitamins
- minerals.

Two other important components of a diet are fibre and water.

The process of digestion allows nutrients to be absorbed by the body. Once in the body, they are used to provide energy and to supply what is needed for the growth and repair of tissues.

How can you know how much of each food you should eat?

How can you know which foods are good for you?

How can you know which foods are not good for you?

These are questions that we will be trying to answer in this unit.

FIG 1.1 There are many different foods to choose from

FIG 1.2 Food enters the body through the mouth and passes into the digestive system

The digestive system

There are different parts to the digestive system. Each part plays an important role in the digestive process.

Some stages of digestion involve physical processes, such as breaking up food in the mouth by the action of chewing. Other stages involve chemical changes brought on by the action of chemicals called enzymes.

Diet and body weight

A person's body weight is affected by various different factors including the types and amounts of food that they eat. People come in all shapes and sizes and many are very healthy and happy. However, there is strong scientific evidence to suggest that being too thin or too fat is not good for you.

If a person eats more energy-providing foods than their body needs, the excess is stored as fat.

FIG 1.3 Exercise requires energy, so one way of burning up unwanted fat is regular exercising

Some people have jobs that are physically demanding so they get their exercise while working. Other people may have jobs in which they sit behind a desk all day. They might need regular sessions in the local gym.

In this unit you will learn how people can stay healthy by finding a balance between the amount of food they eat and the amount of exercise they take.

Challenge

To what extent does the type of food you eat, and the amounts of food you eat, determine your lifestyle?

Or is it your lifestyle that affects the types of food you eat?

Is there a conflict between eating a healthy diet and eating the things you like best?

Food groups

We are learning how to:

- recognise the importance of a balanced diet
- recognise foods from different groups and know how our bodies use them.

Food groups »»

Different foods have different tastes and give us different nutrients that are important to our growth and well-being.

'Go' foods

'Go' foods provide the body with energy.

Foods such as bread, pasta, rice and potatoes, and foods that contain sugar, such as sweets and biscuits, are all sources of **carbohydrates**.

Oils and **fats**, and foods containing them, such as butter and cheese, are also sources of energy for the body.

If you eat more carbohydrates and fats than your body needs, the extra is stored as fat under the skin around the body. Fat is often stored around the waist.

FIG 1.4 Rice is an example of a 'go' food

'Grow' foods

'Grow' foods provide the body with the chemicals it needs to grow by making new cells and tissues.

Foods such as meat and nuts are rich in substances called **proteins**. During digestion, proteins are broken down into chemicals called amino acids.

Amino acids are important because they are needed to make new cells and tissues, and to repair damaged tissues.

FIG 1.5 Palm oil provides the body with oils

FIG 1.6 Meat and nuts are examples of 'grow' foods

FIG 1.7 Fruits and vegetables are rich in vitamins and minerals

1.2

'Glow' foods

'Glow' foods contain important nutrients that you need to stay healthy. Fruits and vegetables are examples of 'glow' foods.

Fruits and vegetables are good sources of two groups of nutrients called **minerals** and **vitamins**, which are essential for remaining healthy. The amounts needed are much less than carbohydrates, fats and proteins.

Fruits and vegetables are also good sources of **fibre**. Fibre does not provide nourishment but it adds bulk to the food so that it can be pushed along the alimentary canal by muscle contraction during digestion. Fibre can also absorb some poisonous waste from food and prevent constipation.

Most foods contain a range of nutrients. Some foods are rich in one particular nutrient.

Activity 1.1

Writing a menu

This activity shows you how to plan your diet to include different types of food.

Here is what you should do:

1. Write a menu for yourself for a day.

2. You should have three meals. Over the day, eat a mixture of 'go', 'grow' and 'glow' foods.

Check your understanding

1. **a)** List the functions of carbohydrates, fats and proteins.

   b) Name three good sources of each type of food.

Fun fact

Minerals containing calcium are essential for the growth of bones and teeth, while iron is needed to make new red blood cells.

Vitamin A helps you to have good eyesight and healthy skin, and vitamin C helps with tissue repair and resistance to disease.

Key terms

carbohydrates foods that provide energy for the body

fats foods that provide energy for the body and store energy for the body to use later

proteins foods that are essential for growth and repair of body tissues

minerals substances that help to build strong bones and teeth, control body fluids and turn the food you eat into energy

vitamins substances that are essential for the body to work properly

fibre a part of the food you eat that the body cannot digest and which consists mainly of cellulose

A balanced diet

We are learning how to:

- recognise the importance of a balanced diet
- create a balanced diet.

Balancing your diet >>>

To stay healthy you need to provide the body with all the different nutrients by eating foods from each food group every day. Altogether, the food you eat is called your **diet**. A **balanced diet** contains all the foods in the correct proportions that you need to stay healthy.

FIG 1.8 You should eat food from each of the food groups every day but you need more food from some groups than from others

For example, if on a particular day, you ate twice as much carbohydrate as normal but no protein, you might be eating the same amount of food, but your body would not obtain the protein it needs for growth and repair.

Nutritional information

Many food packages carry information about the contents of the food on a **nutritional information** panel. You can use this information to help you balance your intake of different nutrients.

NUTRITION

TYPICAL VALUES	PER 100 g SERVING (1/10 OF THE PACK)	
Energy value (Calories)	1480 kJ (350 kcal)	
Protein	9 g	MEDIUM
Carbohydrate	76 g	HIGH
(of which sugars)	(0.4 g)	LOW
Fat	1 g	LOW
(of which saturates)	(0.3 g)	LOW
Fibre	1 g	LOW
Sodium	Trace g	LOW

GUIDELINE DAILY AMOUNTS

Each 100 g serving provides 350 calories, 1 gram of fat and no salt.
Use the following table as a daily guideline:

Each day	Women	Men
Calories	2000	2500
Fat	70 g	95 g
Salt	5 g	7 g

If you eat fewer or more calories, adjust the fat and salt accordingly.

FIG 1.9 Nutritional information label

Analysing my diet

You do not need any equipment or materials for this activity.
Here is what you should do:

1. Copy Table 1.1.

Meal	'Go' food	'Grow' food	'Glow' food
Breakfast			
Lunch			
Dinner			

TABLE 1.1

2. Think about what you had to eat yesterday. For each meal, write down in your table the five foods that you ate most of.

3. Alongside each food, place ticks to show whether it is mainly a 'go', a 'grow' or a 'glow' food. Each food should get five ticks. If you think the food is all in one group, then all five ticks go to that group. If you think the food is a mixture of two or even three groups, then allocate the ticks accordingly. Add any snacks you had during the day to the table as well.

4. From which group did you eat most foods?

5. From which group did you eat fewest foods?

Check your understanding

1. Look at Fig 1.9 again.

   a) Make a list of the nutrients present in this food.

   b) Is this food most likely to be cheese, meat or rice? Explain your answer.

Fun fact

The energy content of food is expressed both in kilojoules (kJ) and in kilocalories (kcal). One calorie is equivalent to 4.18 joules.

The calorie is the old unit of energy. It is where terms like 'calorific value' and 'calorie counter' come from.

Key terms

diet the food you eat

balanced diet a diet that contains all the different nutrients that our body needs to stay healthy

nutritional information information about the nutrients contained in a food

Diet, activity and age

We are learning how to:

- recognise the importance of a balanced diet
- appreciate how diet relates to activity and age.

Diet, activity and age »»

Energy needs

To keep your body working, you need to obtain **energy** from your food. You need energy to breathe, to keep your heart beating and to drive the countless chemical processes that go on all the time throughout your body.

The rate at which these processes take place is called the **basal metabolic rate** (BMR). BMR depends on age and gender, so it varies from person to person. A typical value for an adult is 7000 kJ per day. The total amount of energy a person needs each day will be the sum of their BMR plus additional energy related to how active they are (**activity-related energy**).

total energy needed = BMR + activity-related energy

People who do manual work need a considerable amount of activity-related energy. They need to eat 'go' foods, which are rich in carbohydrates, to give them energy.

Working at a desk all day requires much less activity-related energy. Workers who sit down most of the day need to eat fewer 'go' foods than manual workers.

People who are still growing need 'grow' foods that contain proteins to build new tissues. A fully grown person only needs proteins to repair existing tissues. Teenagers need more 'grow' foods than adults.

FIG 1.10 Some people's jobs require a lot more energy than others

FIG 1.11 A person who is growing needs more 'grow' foods than a person who is fully grown

A pregnant woman needs a healthy, balanced diet to ensure that her unborn child has all the nutrients it needs to develop.

'Glow' foods such as fruit and vegetables keep us healthy. People sometimes do not eat enough 'glow' foods.

Activity 1.3

Advising people on their diet

This activity is a role play in which people are given advice about their diets.

1. Choose one student who is going to be the dietician. This is a professional person who advises people about their diets.

2. The remaining students will pretend to be people of different ages with different occupations, for example a 20-year-old shop assistant or a 70-year-old retired person.

3. Each person should think of some difficult questions to ask the dietician.

4. The dietician should give each person advice about their diet according to their activity and age.

5. Swap roles so that everyone in the group gets a turn at being the dietician.

FIG 1.12 Everyone should eat several portions of fruit and vegetables each day no matter what job they do or how old they are

Check your understanding

1. Table 1.2 shows the amount of energy required each day by three people: A, B and C.

Person	Amount of energy required each day /kJ
A	15 000
B	9 500
C	11 000

TABLE 1.2

a) Which of these people is likely to be:
   i)   a teenage girl?
   ii) an office worker?
   iii) a labourer on a building site?

b) Estimate the amount of energy that person A needs each day as a result of their job.

Fun fact

The amount of energy different foods contain is measured by a food calorimeter. A known mass of the food is burned in oxygen and the amount of heat produced is measured.

Key terms

energy what the body needs to function, usually obtained from food

basal metabolic rate rate at which the basic functions of the body, such as breathing, heart beating, take place

activity-related energy energy related to how active a person is

The digestive system (1)

We are learning how to:

- outline the basic structure of the digestive system and the functions of each part
- identify parts of the digestive system.

Getting digestion started ❯❯❯

The **digestive system** obtains nutrients and water from the foods that we eat.

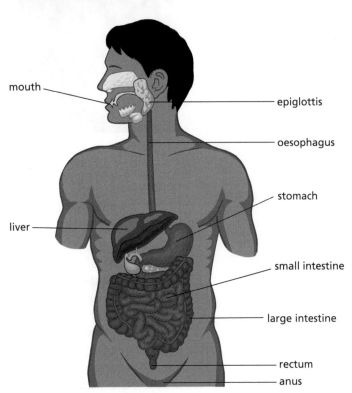

FIG 1.13 The digestive system

Digestion begins in the **mouth**. Food is chopped into smaller pieces by the pointed teeth and crushed by the flat teeth. Breaking the food into smaller pieces allows digestive enzymes to penetrate it more easily.

It is important to keep our teeth clean and healthy.

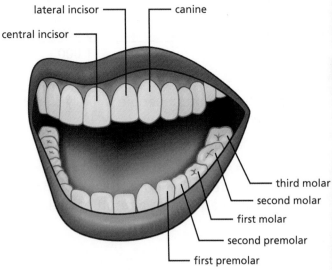

FIG 1.14 There are four different kinds of teeth in our mouths

Activity 1.4

Investigating teeth

Here is what you need:

- toothbrush
- toothpaste
- small mirror.

Here is what you should do:

1. Clean your teeth before starting this investigation.

2. Look carefully at the teeth right at the front of your mouth. What shape are they?

3. Draw a picture showing the shape.

4. By thinking about the shape, can you suggest what job this kind of tooth does?

5. Look along your front teeth to the side of the mouth until you see a tooth that is a different shape.

6. Draw a picture showing the shape.

7. By thinking about the shape, can you say what job this kind of tooth does?

8. Look at the teeth at the back of your mouth.

9. Draw a picture showing the shape.

10. By thinking about the shape, can you say what job this kind of tooth does?

In addition to wetting food and making it easier to swallow, the saliva released in the mouth also contains enzymes known as **carbohydrases**. These are digestive enzymes that break down carbohydrates into simple sugars – such as glucose – that can easily be absorbed by the body.

Check your understanding

1. Look carefully at these two teeth.

   State what type each tooth is and explain how the shape of each tooth is suited to its role in digestion.

a) 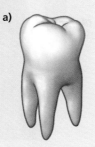 b)

FIG 1.15

Key terms

digestive system the parts of the body that work together to process the food you eat

mouth where food enters the digestive system

carbohydrases enzymes that break down carbohydrates in foods

The digestive system (2)

We are learning how to:

- outline the basic structure of the digestive system and the functions of each part
- identify parts of the digestive system.

Moving digestion along ⟩⟩

When you swallow, food from the mouth passes down the oesophagus into the **stomach**.

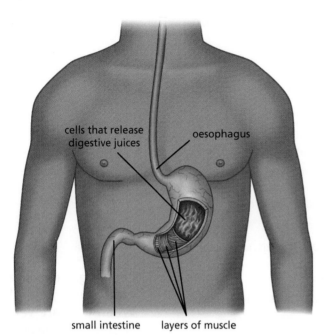

FIG 1.16 The stomach is a muscular bag that is about the size of your fist when empty but can expand to ten times this size when full of food

> **Fun fact**
>
> The epiglottis is a small flap of cartilage in the throat. When you swallow it moves down and blocks the entrance to the larynx so that food is directed down the oesophagus.

The wall of the stomach contains cells that release digestive juices. These include hydrochloric acid which makes the stomach very acidic. Stomach juices also contain enzymes called **proteases**. These enzymes act on proteins, breaking them down into chemicals called peptides.

The movement of the stomach muscles continues to break up the food and mixes it as digestive enzymes are added.

The **small intestine** is about seven metres long in an adult. The digesting food passes into the small intestine from the stomach and is moved along it by the rhythmic contraction of the muscular walls. This rhythmic contraction is called peristalsis.

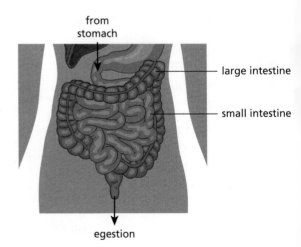

FIG 1.17 The intestines

In the first part of the small intestine – the duodenum – the cells produce enzymes that continue to break down the food. In addition to carbohydrases and proteases, the cells also produces a third group of enzymes called **lipases** which break down fats.

Digestion continues in the second part of the small intestine – the ileum – and this is also where most of the absorption of nutrients takes place.

The wall of the ileum is lined with finger-like projections called villi. Together they provide a large surface area for absorption. Each villus has its own blood supply. The villi walls are very thin so the products of digestion can easily pass into the blood stream.

The **large intestine** is about 1.5 metres long in an adult. No further absorption of nutrients takes place in the large intestine. It has the important function of absorbing water back into the body.

The remains of the food in the large intestine contain mostly cellulose from plants. The body cannot digest these remains. They are egested from the body as faeces.

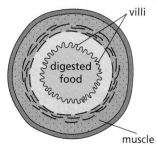

FIG 1.18 Cross-section of small intestine

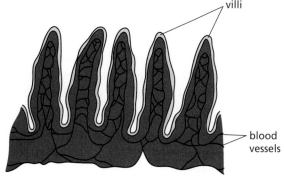

FIG 1.19 Villi cross-section

Activity 1.5

Looking at a model of the digestive system

Here is what you need:

- model of the digestive system.

Here is what you should do:

1. Look carefully at the model. Identify the different parts that have been described.

2. Try to visualise where the various parts are in your body.

Check your understanding

1. In which part of the digestive system:

   a) is food chopped into small pieces and crushed?

   b) is water reabsorbed?

   c) does most absorption of nutrients take place?

   d) is acid added to the food?

   e) does the chemical breakdown of food start?

Key terms

stomach muscular bag-like organ, a part of the digestive system, where food is mixed with enzymes

proteases enzymes that break down proteins in food

small intestine the part of the digestive system where food is broken down further and nutrients are absorbed

lipases enzymes that break down fats in food

large intestine the part of the digestive system where water is absorbed back into the body

The process of digestion

We are learning how to:

- explain how humans obtain nutrients from food
- describe the physical and chemical changes in food during digestion.

Breaking down food ⟫

During digestion food goes through both **physical changes** and **chemical changes**.

- The physical changes involve breaking the food down into small pieces through biting, chewing in the mouth and crushing in the stomach.

- The chemical changes involve the action of enzymes to break the large molecules in food into smaller molecules that can be absorbed easily by the body.

Both sets of processes are important. Biting and chewing the food does not release nutrients in food, but it does turn the food into a form in which chemical reactions can take place more efficiently.

Activity 1.6

Particle size and the rate of a chemical reaction

Your teacher will carry this out as a demonstration.

Here is what you need:

- balance
- 250 cm³ beaker
- measuring cylinder
- stopwatch
- limestone – one large lump of mass about 2 g
- calcium carbonate – fine powder
- hydrochloric acid of concentration 1 mol dm⁻³.

 SAFETY
Be careful when using acid. Follow local regulations.

Here is what you should do:

1. Weigh your lump of limestone (limestone is an impure form of calcium carbonate). It should be about 2 g.

2. Place the limestone in a 250 cm³ beaker.

3. Measure 100 cm³ of hydrochloric acid of concentration 1 mol dm⁻³ in the measuring cylinder.

4. Add the hydrochloric acid to the beaker and start the stopwatch at the same time.

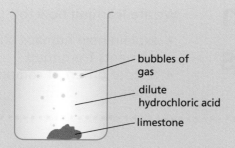

FIG 1.20 Limestone in hydrochloric acid

5. Continue observing and timing until the reaction is complete. This will be when all of the limestone has dissolved and no more bubbles are given off.

6. Weigh out the same mass of calcium carbonate powder as the mass of your piece of limestone.

7. Repeat steps 2 to 5.

8. Copy and complete Table 1.3 with your results.

Form of calcium carbonate	Appearance	Time taken for reaction to reach completion
single piece	large lump	
fine	powder	

TABLE 1.3

9. What evidence is there from your observations that breaking food into smaller pieces will increase the rate at which enzymes can break it down?

Not only does chewing food into small pieces make it easier to swallow but it also makes it easier for digestive enzymes to act on the food.

Check your understanding

1. Fig 1.21 shows two different sorts of sugar.

a)  b)

FIG 1.21

If equal masses of the sugar were added to cups of coffee and stirred, which sugar would dissolve first? Explain your answer.

Key terms

physical changes
changes that take place as a result of physical processes such as chewing

chemical changes
changes that take place as a result of chemical reactions such as action of enzymes on food

Food tests – starch and simple sugars

We are learning how to:

- explain how humans obtain nutrients from food
- test for different components in foods.

Food tests >>>

Food can be tested for carbohydrates, either in the form of **starch** or as **simple sugars** such as glucose.

Testing for starch

You might recall the test for starch from the work you carried out in Form 1 on photosynthesis.

When a few drops of **iodine solution** are added to a food containing starch, it turns a blue-black colour.

Testing for simple sugars

To test for the presence of a simple sugar, place a small sample of the food into a test tube containing **Benedict's reagent**. Heat the test tube for a few minutes in a hot water bath. If a simple sugar is present, the mixture will turn brick red.

FIG 1.23 Positive test for the presence of starch

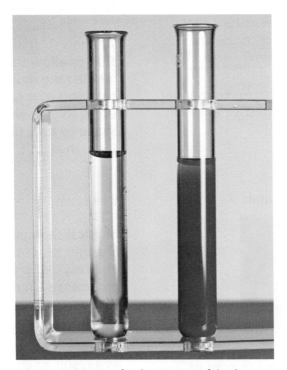

FIG 1.24 Positive test for the presence of simple sugars. The test tube on the left contains Benedict's reagent and the one on the right shows Benedict's reagent with a simple sugar after heating

Testing for starch and simple sugars

Here is what you need:

- Biuret reagent
- starch solution
- Benedict's reagent
- iodine
- water
- test tubes
- water bath
- food samples.

⚠️ **SAFETY**
Be careful when using chemicals. Follow local regulations.

Here is what you should do:

1. Your teacher will provide you with samples of some foods.

2. Test each food for the presence of starch and simple sugars.

3. Arrange your results in a table like Table 1.4. Place a tick or a cross in each column next to each food as appropriate.

Food sample	Starch present	Simple sugars present

TABLE 1.4

Check your understanding

1. You drop some iodine onto a food sample. The food sample turns blue-black. What does this tell you about the food?

2. How could you find out whether the food sample contains glucose?

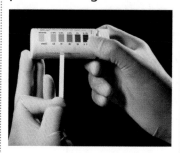
Key terms

starch a form of carbohydrate found in foods

simple sugars a form of carbohydrate found in foods

iodine solution a solution containing iodine that is used to test for starch

Benedict's reagent a chemical used to test for the presence of simple sugars such as glucose

Food tests – proteins and fats

We are learning how to:

- explain how humans obtain nutrients from food
- test for different components in foods.

Food tests >>>

You can use food tests to find out which particular food components are present in different foods.

Testing for proteins

Biuret reagent is a mixture of sodium hydroxide solution and copper(II) sulfate solution. It is used to test for **proteins**.

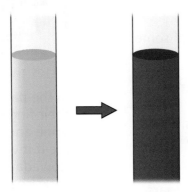

FIG 1.26 Positive test for the presence of proteins

When a sample of food is added to Biuret reagent, the reagent changes colour from blue to purple if protein is present.

Testing for fats

Fats are soluble in **ethanol** but insoluble in water. This provides a simple way to test for fats.

When a sample of food is shaken in a test tube with a small amount of ethanol, any fat it contains will dissolve in the ethanol.

If water is then added to the ethanol, any fat present comes out of solution as tiny globules that cause the ethanol to become cloudy.

FIG 1.27 Positive test for the presence of fats, note the cloudiness in the liquid at the top of the tube

Activity 1.8

Testing for proteins and fats

Here is what you need:

- Biuret reagent
- ethanol
- water
- test tube
- water bath
- food samples.

⚠️ **SAFETY**
Be careful when using chemicals. Follow local regulations.

Here is what you should do:

1. Your teacher will provide you with samples of some foods.

2. Test each food for the presence of proteins and fats.

3. Arrange your results in a table like Table 1.5. Place a tick or a cross in each column next to each food as appropriate.

Food sample	Protein present	Fat present

TABLE 1.5

Check your understanding

1. A food gives positive tests with Biuret reagent and ethanol/water but negative tests with iodine solution and Benedict's solution.

   a) Which components are present in the food?
   b) Which components are absent from the food?
   c) Suggest what the food might be.

Key terms

Biuret reagent a mixture of sodium hydroxide solution and copper(II) sulfate solution used to test for the presence of proteins in food

proteins a food group

fats a food group

ethanol a chemical in which fat dissolves

Energy values in food

We are learning how to:

- explain how humans obtain nutrients from food
- assess the energy values of different foods.

How much energy is in your food? 》》

The amount of energy a food provides the body with is sometimes called its **calorific value**. The calorie is the old term for a unit of energy. It depends on the proportion of carbohydrates and fats the food contains. Carbohydrates and fats can be converted to energy by the body.

One method for finding out how much energy a food contains is to burn a sample and use the energy that is produced to heat a known mass of water. The temperature increase of the water can be used to calculate the amount of energy released.

Activity 1.9

The calorific value of peanuts

Here is what you need:

- peanut (your teacher might substitute a different food)
- stand and clamp
- thermometer
- water
- boiling tube
- measuring cylinder
- Bunsen burner
- mounting needle.

⚠️ **SAFETY**

Take care when using a Bunsen burner. If you have a nut allergy you should advise your teacher and you should not carry out this activity.

Here is what you should do:

1. Measure 50 cm³ of water and pour it into a boiling tube.

2. Support the boiling tube with a stand and clamp.

3. Measure the temperature of the water.

4. Push the end of a mounting needle into a peanut.

5. Hold the peanut in the flame of a Bunsen burner just until it starts to burn.

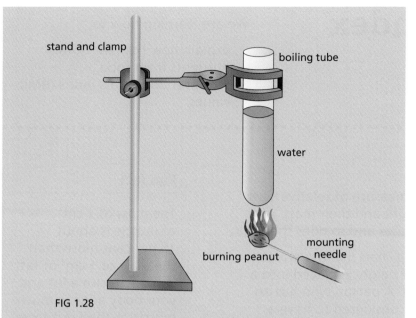

FIG 1.28

6. Hold the burning peanut under the boiling tube and keep it there until it stops burning. (If the peanut goes out accidentally, relight it from the Bunsen flame.)

7. As soon as the peanut has stopped burning, measure the temperature of the water.

8. By how many degrees did the temperature of the water increase?

9. It takes 209 J of energy to raise the temperature of 50 cm³ of water by 1 °C. Use this information to calculate how much energy was given out by the burning peanut.

> **Fun fact**
>
> On some food packaging you will see that kilocalorie is written as calorie, so 10 calories actually means 10 kilocalories.

> **Key term**
>
> **calorific value** the amount of energy that the body can obtain from a food

The amount of energy that the body obtains by eating a portion of a food is often shown on the packaging.

Check your understanding

1. Fig 1.29 shows details about the composition of white bread.

   a) From which components of the food does the body get most energy?

   b) How much energy, in kilojoules, would be in two slices of bread used to make a sandwich?

   c) A loaf contains 7880 kJ of energy. What is the mass of the loaf of white bread?

NUTRITION

Typical values	100 g contains	Each slice (typically 44 g) contains
Energy	985 kJ	435 kJ
	235 kcal	105 kcal
Fat	1.5 g	0.7 g
of which saturates	0.3 g	0.1 g
Carbohydrate	45.5 g	20.0 g
of which sugars	3.8 g	1.7 g
Fibre	2.8 g	1.2 g
Protein	7.7 g	3.4 g
Salt	1.0 g	0.4 g

FIG 1.29

Body mass index

We are learning how to:

- explain how humans obtain nutrients from food
- interpret body mass index (BMI) values.

Finding your BMI

The **body mass index (BMI)** is a measure of relative size, which is based on a person's height and their mass. As a person grows, their height increases and so does their mass.

The BMI is often represented as a chart like the one in Fig 1.30. A person of a particular height is placed into a category according to their mass. A person who has an average mass for their height is considered to have a normal BMI. If they are under this mass they are **underweight**, and it they are over this mass they are **overweight**, or even **obese**.

> **Fun fact**
>
> The mass of 1 cm³ of muscle is about 15 per cent more than the mass of 1 cm³ of fat. If you exercise a lot and your body adds as much muscle as the fat it loses, your body mass will actually increase.

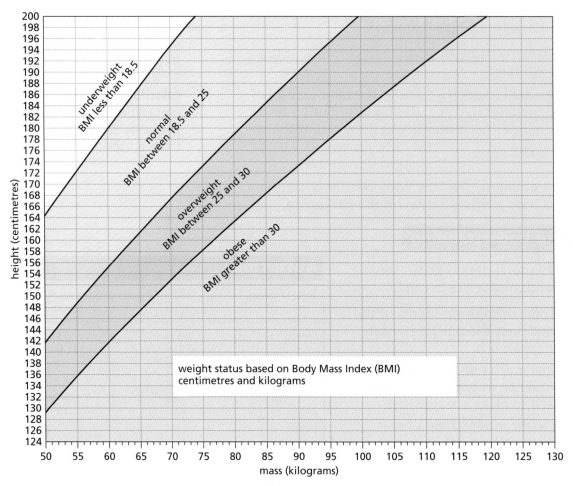

FIG 1.30 BMI chart

Care should be taken when applying BMI to health and fitness because it takes no account of a person's build or the amount of muscle they have.

Activity 1.10

Finding where you are on the BMI chart

You should work with a partner on this activity.

Here is what you need:

- measuring tape
- bathroom scales.

Here is what you should do:

1. Stand upright with your back to a wall.

2. Ask your partner to mark with a finger the position on the wall where the top of your head reaches.

3. Measure your height in centimetres as the distance from their finger to the floor.

4. Write down your height in centimetres.

5. Take your shoes off and stand on the bathroom scales.

6. Make sure the scales are set to kilograms and read off your mass.

7. Write down your mass in kilograms.

8. On Fig 1.30, place your left index finger on your height and your right index finger on your mass. Bring your fingers across and up until they meet. In what part of the chart is your BMI?

FIG 1.31 The BMI of a sportsperson might suggest that they are obese because their bodies carry lots of muscle, which increases their mass; however, they are not obese

Check your understanding

1. Kelvin is 178 cm tall and has a mass of 91 kg.

    a) In what category of the BMI chart is he?

    b) In what range is his BMI?

    c) How much mass would he need to lose to move into the normal category?

2. Angel is 174 cm tall and has a mass of 51 kg.

    a) In what category of the BMI chart is she?

    b) In what range is her BMI?

    c) What advice would you give Angel about her diet and eating habits?

Key terms

body mass index (BMI) a measure of relative size that is based on a person's height and mass

underweight a BMI of less than 18.5

overweight a BMI between 25 and 30

obese a BMI of over 30

Weight gain and loss

We are learning how to:

- relate diet to weight gain and loss
- account for changes to the body when we eat too much.

Changing weight ›››

Everything you eat is broken down in the digestive system and the nutrients are either used or stored for future use.

If you eat more 'go' foods (carbohydrates and fats) than your body needs, the nutrients are stored as fat. This is why some people become overweight. If a person who is overweight continues to eat more 'go' foods than they need, they will become obese.

Although the joule is the modern unit of energy, the calorie is still widely used in relation to diet. Foods can be classified as **high-calorie** or **low-calorie**.

As discussed earlier in the unit, the amount of nutrients a person needs each day is linked to their level of activity.

FIG 1.32 Carbohydrates and fats that the body does not use are stored as fat

FIG 1.33 People who have jobs that are not physically demanding need to limit the amount of calories they eat and take regular exercise if they want to avoid becoming overweight

As people grow old and retire from work they often become less active. They may not be able to compensate for this by taking more exercise.

It is not just a question of how much food a person eats but also what foods they eat. Low-calorie foods contain less energy than other foods and can help a person to reduce their body mass.

FIG 1.34 Older people need to reduce the amount of calories they eat to what their body needs to remain healthy

FIG 1.35 A meal of low-calorie foods

1.12

Activity 1.11

Exploring a low-calorie meal

You will not need any equipment or materials for this activity.

Here is what you should do:

1. Look carefully at the meal shown in Fig 1.35.

2. Make a list of all of the low-calorie foods you can see.

3. Carry out some research to find some more low-calorie foods.

Check your understanding

1. Here are some low-calorie meals from a café menu.

Breakfast meals	Lunch meals	Dinner meals	Snacks
The Power Breakfast Smoothie **308 calories**	Burrito **308 calories**	Tomato, Spinach and Chickpea Stew **265 calories**	1 Piece of Fruit or 1/2 cup of Berries **80–100 calories**
The Chocolate Smoothie **270 calories**	Sausage and Salad **315 calories**	Vegan Veggie and "Bacon" Pizza **272 calories**	10 Almonds and 1/2 cup Strawberries **92 calories**
Protein and Oatmeal Recipe **294 calories**	Couscous Salad **295 calories**	Vegetarian Lentil Chilli **256 calories**	2 tbsp of Baba Ganoush 1/2 cup Sliced Carrots **94 calories**
Chia Pudding **266 calories**	Chestnut and Vegetable Vegetarian Stew **265 calories**	Shrimp and Quinoa Dinner **308 calories**	2 tbsp Spicy Hummus Flatbread **125 calories**
Hot and Cold Simple Breakfast Plate **277 calories**	Thai Salad Rolls **298 calories**	The Super Salad **297 calories**	1 tbsp of Natural Peanut Butter and 1/2 cup Celery **125 calories**

FIG 1.36

a) Suggest meals for a day for someone who wants to lose mass by eating low-calorie food.

b) Count up the total number of calories in your meal suggestions.

Fun fact

Sumo wrestlers in Japan may have a body mass of hundreds of kilograms. They train very hard and eat up to 10 000 calories each day. This is about five times the amount of food eaten by the average man.

FIG 1.37 Sumo wrestler

When a sumo wrestler retires he becomes much less active. He must, therefore, drastically reduce the number of calories he eats each day.

Key terms

high-calorie food containing high number of calories per portion

low-calorie food containing low number of calories per portion

Fat or thin?

We are learning how to:

- explain why some people are naturally fat or thin
- relate body weight and diet to lifestyle.

Genetic disposition ▶▶

A person's physical features are determined by **genetic information** passed on by their father and their mother. This is why children generally look like their parents.

In any population there is variation, and humans are no different than any other organisms in this respect. Some people are naturally taller or more heavily built than others.

If you have parents who are large and well-built, then it is likely that you will also be this shape. To some extent your diet will be determined by the calories and nutrients you need to attain and maintain your natural body shape.

Conversely, if your parents are slightly built and have a low body mass, then it is likely that you will be similar in size and shape to them. Your body might require fewer calories and nutrients than a larger person.

FIG 1.38 People come in different sizes

Lifestyle ▶▶

A person's **lifestyle** is the way in which they live. It is determined by the choices they make, irrespective of their natural body shape.

We already learned in the previous topic how dietary requirements are linked to a person's occupation. The link between activity and diet is not limited to jobs but to everything we do in our lives.

Journeys in which we walk or cycle need lots more energy than when we are driven in a car or bus.

Activities like video games might be fun to play but they don't require much energy. Your body will use a lot more energy dancing at the local disco.

In general, the more active we are, the more energy and nutrients our bodies need.

FIG 1.39 Which means of getting to school needs more energy: cycling or being driven?

FIG 1.40 Which activity needs more energy: video games or disco dancing?

Activity 1.12

Does my lifestyle match my diet?

Work in a group of three or four students.

Here is what you should do:

1. Make a list of the activities you carry out each day as part of your lifestyle. For example, you might ask yourself questions like:

a) How do I get to and from school?

b) What do I do at break time and lunchtime?

c) What do I do after school?

d) How do I spend my leisure time in the evening?

2. Alongside each activity, write how much energy your body needs to carry it out. Score it on a scale from 1 to 5 where '1' needs least energy and '5' needs most energy.

3. Decide how well your diet matches your overall level of activity. Do you think that maybe:

a) you eat a little more than your lifestyle requires?

b) you eat about the right amount for your lifestyle?

c) you should eat a little more to keep up with your lifestyle?

4. Discuss your activity–lifestyle balance with the other students in your group.

Check your understanding

1. Here is a summary of a survey carried out by the Caribbean Food and Nutrition Institute and the Trinidad and Tobago Olympic Committee.

Overall, the survey showed high rates of obesity throughout the Island. The health minister, Dr Fuad Khan, states that the study focused on children in rural areas and that it would be frightening if one examined the statistics of child obesity in urban areas.

The Health Ministry and the Education Ministry together aim to change the meals distributed to pupils in the school feeding programme.

Dr Khan added that tackling child obesity was a difficult task as it needed the full support of parents.

Dr Khan further said that the expanding fast-food industry, and in particular the use of chemicals in these foods to make them addictive, was one of the problems.

a) Which type of food was identified as being a problem?

b) Suggest why is it likely that obesity will be even more of a problem in urban areas than in rural areas?

c) Why might some parents not give full support to tackling this problem?

d) How might the contents of meals provided in the school feeding programme change?

> **Fun fact**
>
> A recent survey of school-aged children (5–18 years) in Trinidad and Tobago found that 25% were overweight or obese.

Key terms

genetic information information passed on from parent to offspring carried in the chromosomes of sex cells

lifestyle the choices we make about what we do and how we live our lives

Health and diet

We are learning how to:

- relate diet to weight gain and loss
- avoid health problems through a sensible diet.

Health and diet ⟫⟫

Doctors have discovered that being overweight can affect a person's health. Here are some conditions that are believed to be linked to being overweight or obese.

- **Heart disease** – The coronary arteries supply the heart with oxygen-rich blood. In **coronary heart disease**, a waxy plaque builds up inside the walls of the arteries and reduces the flow of blood. This may lead to chest pains – angina – and can cause a heart attack.

  Obesity may also cause heart failure when the heart cannot pump enough blood for the needs of the body.

- **High blood pressure (hypertension)** – Blood pressure is the force with which blood is pushed through the arteries by the heart. If the arteries become narrower, as a result of plaque deposits, the blood pressure will rise. This can damage the body in many ways.

- **Stroke** – As a result of the build-up of plaque, an artery may eventually rupture, causing a blood clot to form. A clot close to the brain can block the flow of blood and reduce the amount of oxygen the brain receives. This causes a **stroke**.

- **Type 2 diabetes** – Normally, the body breaks down carbohydrates into glucose, which is then carried to the cells throughout the body. Any excess glucose is stored. In **type 2 diabetes**, the body cannot control its blood sugar level and it becomes far higher than it should be, leading to other problems, including heart disease, and damage to the nervous system and the kidneys.

- **Cancer** – Being obese raises the risk of colon, breast and other types of **cancer**.

FIG 1.41 Heart disease may result in pains to the chest and a heart attack

Problems associated with eating patterns

Most people have a regular pattern for eating their meals. Their bodies get used to this pattern of eating and digestion. However, this is not possible for some groups of people, such as shift workers.

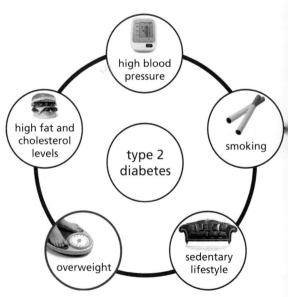

high blood pressure

high fat and cholesterol levels

smoking

type 2 diabetes

sedentary lifestyle

overweight

FIG 1.42 Being overweight is one of the factors thought to increase the risk of type 2 diabetes

FIG 1.43 Shift workers

Shift workers who work until late in the day or even through the night may eat their meals at different times from most people. When they are off work they eat their meals at normal times.

Scientists have found that changes in eating patterns are bad for the body. Shift workers are generally less healthy and more inclined to become overweight than people with regular day jobs.

Activity 1.13

Eating patterns

1. Write down your eating pattern for a typical day. At what times do you generally have your meals?

2. Imagine you are working shifts from 8:00 p.m. to 6:00 a.m. Write down an eating pattern for a typical working day.

3. What problems do you foresee at the end of your working week when you change over to a normal eating pattern?

Check your understanding

1. Explain each of the following statements.

   a) A build-up of plaque in the coronary artery may lead to a heart attack.

   b) Type 2 diabetes is caused to some extent by bad choices in lifestyle.

Key terms

coronary heart disease a condition where plaque builds up inside the walls of the arteries and reduces the flow of blood

stroke when a blood clot blocks the flow of blood to the brain

type 2 diabetes when the body cannot control its blood sugar level and it becomes far higher than it should be

cancer a condition in which cells in the body change and grow in an uncontrolled way causing a tumour

Review of Diet and health

- 'Go' foods are rich in carbohydrates, which give the body energy.

- 'Grow' foods are rich in proteins, which the body needs to make new cells and repair damaged tissue.

- 'Glow' foods are rich in vitamins and minerals, which the body needs in small amounts.

- A balanced diet is one that contains sufficient, but not an excess of, all of the nutrients a person needs to remain healthy.

- Fibre or roughage has no nutritional value but it is an important component of the diet because it gives digesting food bulk, so it can be pushed along the alimentary canal.

- A person's diet should be related to their age and their level of activity.

- The basal metabolic rate, or BMR, is what a person needs to keep alive, even when they are at rest.

- The digestive system obtains nutrients and water from the foods that we eat.

- Digestion takes place in the alimentary canal. This consists of the mouth, oesophagus, stomach, small intestine and large intestine.

- Food is physically broken into pieces and crushed in the mouth by the act of chewing.

- Food is chemically broken down by chemicals called enzymes.

- Most absorption of nutrients takes place in the small intestine.

- Absorption of water takes place in the large intestine.

- Incisor and canine teeth are found at the front of the mouth. Their job is to cut and tear food into pieces.

- Premolar and molar teeth are found at the back of the mouth. Their job is to crush food.

Food tests

Food test for:	Reagent	Positive result
starch	iodine solution	blue-black colour
simple sugars	Benedict's reagent	blue to brick red
proteins	Biuret reagent	blue to purple
fats	ethanol followed by water	ethanol goes cloudy

TABLE 1.6

- The amount of energy in a food is called its calorific value. This comes from the calorie, which is an old unit of energy.

- Food packaging often contains data about the calorific value of the food as well as detailed information about its composition.

- The body mass index, or BMI, is a measure of relative size, which is based on a person's height and their mass.

- On the basis of their BMI, a person might be classified as underweight, normal, overweight or obese.

- Excess carbohydrates and fats that are not used by the body are stored in the body as fat.

- Different foods have different calorific values. Low-calorie foods are often eaten by people hoping to lose body mass.

- Lifestyle is determined by the choices we make on how to live our lives.

- Excess body mass has been linked to a number of conditions including heart attack, high blood pressure, stroke, type 2 diabetes and some types of cancer.

- Regular changes to eating patterns, such as those made by shift workers, increase the chances of health problems and becoming overweight.

Review questions on Diet and health

1. Copy and complete the following sentences.

   a) A _____ diet is one that contains nutrients in amounts and proportions needed by the body.

   b) People who eat more food than their body needs risk becoming overweight or even _____ .

   c) A person might have a heart attack if their coronary _____ becomes blocked.

   d) When a person suffers from diabetes, their body cannot control their _____ level.

   e) Being overweight may cause extra wear on the _____ and they may become painful as a person moves about.

2. a) Which type of teeth break food into smaller pieces?

   b) Why is the action of these teeth important for the process of digestion?

   c) What is the name of the group of chemicals that breaks food down during digestion?

   d) Name one example from this group of chemicals that acts on proteins.

   e) What nutrients are obtained from the breakdown of proteins?

3. a) What do the letters BMI stand for in the context of diet?

   b) What information does a person's BMI provide?

   c) What action should a person in the 'obese' category take to improve their health? Suggest how they might do this.

4. Fig 1.RQ.1 represents the human digestive system.

a) Which of the labelled parts is the:

i) small intestine?

ii) oesophagus?

b) In which of the labelled parts:

i) does digestion begin?

ii) are most nutrients absorbed?

iii) is acid added to food?

iv) is most water absorbed?

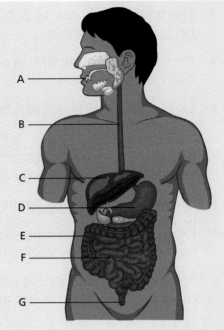

FIG 1.RQ.1

5. Fig 1.RQ.2 shows the nutritional information from a food package.

a) Which of the three nutrient groups, carbohydrates, fats or proteins, does this food have:

i) most of?

ii) least of?

b) What other important constituent of food, which has no nutritional value, does this food contain?

c) By considering the information given, would you say that this food is a cereal, meat or cheese? Explain your answer.

6. a) Give three examples of 'go' foods.

b) How is the job a person does linked to the amount of 'go' foods he or she should eat each day?

c) What group of nutrients do 'go' foods contain?

d) How do 'go' foods provide the body with energy?

e) If a person eats more 'go' foods than their body needs, what happens to the extra nutrients?

TYPICAL VALUES
NUTRITION INFORMATION

	per 100 g	per 40 g	per 40 g***
Energy	1565 kJ/ 374 kcal	626 kJ/ 150 kcal	1222 kJ/ 291 kcal
Protein	11.0 g	4.4 g	8 g
Carbohydrate	60 g	24.0 g	38.4 g
(of which sugars)	1.1 g	0.4 g	14.8 g
Fat	8 g	3.2 g	8.6 g
(of which saturates)	1.5 g	0.6 g	3.9 g
Fibre	9 g	3.6 g	3.6 g
(of which beta glucan)	3.6 g	1.4 g	1.4 g
Sodium**	Trace	Trace	0.1 g
**Equivalent as salt	Trace	Trace	0.3 g

*** with 300 ml of semi skimmed milk

*Each serving (40 g) contains 47% of the 3 g of oat beta glucan suggested per day to help lower cholesterol as part of a varied and balanced diet and healthy lifestyle. Reducing cholesterol helps maintain a healthy heart.

FIG 1.RQ.2

7. a) What substance is iodine solution used to test for?

b) What change would you see when Benedict's reagent is heated with glucose in a water bath?

c) What reagent is used to test for the presence of proteins?

d) Describe how to test a food to find out if it contains fats.

8. Table 1.7 gives some information about 100 g samples of some different foods.

Food	Carbohydrates %	Fats %	Protein %
beef	0	28.2	14.8
bread	52	1.8	9
carrots	5.4	0	0.7
fish	0	0.5	16
jam	69.2	0	0.5
oranges	8.5	0	0.8
peanuts	8.7	49	28.1
potatoes	18	0	2
rice	86.7	1	6

TABLE 1.7

a) Name two other types of nutrient that are not shown in Table 1.7.

b) Which of the foods in Table 1.7 is the richest source of:

   i) carbohydrates?

   ii) proteins?

   iii) fats?

c) Which two of the foods in Table 1.7 should be avoided by someone on a low carbohydrate diet?

d) Vegetarians do not eat meat or fish. Which two of the foods in Table 1.7 provide the best alternative sources of protein?

9. Amy and Matthew sometimes eat at Café 35 near their school.

CAFÉ 35 Lunchtime menu		
Beef burger	Chips	Jam doughnut
Pizza	Jacket potato	Chocolate cake
Salad roll	Pasta	Yoghurt
Sausage roll	Baked beans	Fruit squash
Jamaican pattie	Peas	Milk

a) Matthew is 14 years old. He likes watching sport on the television but he does not play any sport himself. He is a little overweight. He gets a lift to school each day in his parents' car. For his lunch he chose: beef burger, chips, baked beans, jam doughnut and fruit squash.

   Could Matthew have made a better choice? Explain your answer.

b) Amy is 15 years old. She runs cross-country races and plays lots of different sports. She is very fit and cycles to school each day. For her lunch she chose: salad roll, yoghurt and milk.

   Could Amy have made a better choice? Explain your answer.

Unit 2: Human body systems: the circulatory system

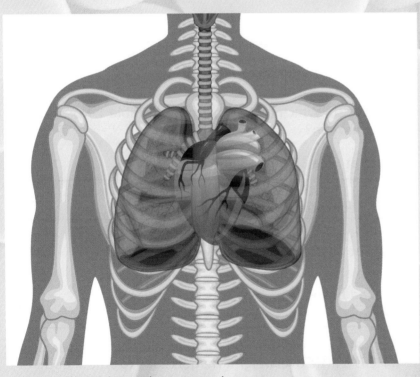

Introduction ⟫

The circulatory system is a series of tubes or vessels that carry blood to all parts of the body. The major components of the circulatory system are the heart and different types of blood vessels. In the blood there are essential substances needed to keep the cells alive and functioning.

Heart

The heart has the job of pumping blood through the circulatory system. It is made of a special kind of muscle that contracts and relaxes constantly, without any rest.

FIG 2.1 Your heart is in your chest near your lungs

Your heart starts to beat before you are born and carries on without stopping until the day you die.

Blood vessels

The circulatory system has different sorts of blood vessels. The vessels that carry blood away from the heart are called arteries and the vessels that carry blood back towards the heart are called veins.

Blood

Blood is a complex mixture of different chemicals and cells. If a sample of blood is spun in a centrifuge for a short time it separates out into a straw-coloured liquid called plasma and a dark red mass of blood cells.

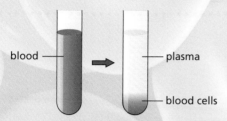

blood — plasma

blood cells

FIG 2.2 Separating blood into plasma and cells

Blood is red because red blood cells contain a pigment called haemoglobin.

Pulse rate

When the heart pushes blood along arteries, it creates a pulse that you can feel at certain points on the body.

Doctors sometimes check a patient's pulse rate as a way of finding out if their heart is functioning normally.

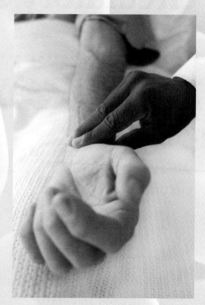

FIG 2.3 Checking a patient's pulse rate

Circulatory problems

If anything goes wrong with the heart or the other parts of the circulatory system, it could be extremely dangerous. Doctors take chest pains very seriously as they could indicate a heart problem.

FIG 2.4 Chest pains

Challenge

When a healthy person dies as a result of an accident, their heart might improve the life of another person. It is possible for a person with a defective heart to receive a heart transplant.

Give Life... Become An Organ Donor

THE MINISTRY OF HEALTH
NATIONAL ORGAN DONOR PROGRAMME

FIG 2.5 National Organ Donor Programme

Do you think that people should become organ donors?

Structure of the circulatory system

We are learning how to:

- outline the basic structure of the circulatory system
- identify different parts of the circulatory system.

The circulatory system ⟩⟩

Activity 2.1

What do I already know about the circulatory system?

You do not need any equipment or materials for this activity.

Here is what you should do:

1. Write down what you already know about the circulatory system. This should include the names of the parts and what you think they do.

The **circulatory system** is a complex network of blood vessels that delivers blood to every cell in the body. At the centre of the network is the **heart**. The purpose of the heart is to pump blood around the blood vessels.

The human circulatory system can be described as a **double circulatory system** because it has two circuits, or parts, to it.

In one circuit, blood passes between the heart and the lungs. While in the lungs, blood absorbs oxygen and releases carbon dioxide and water vapour.

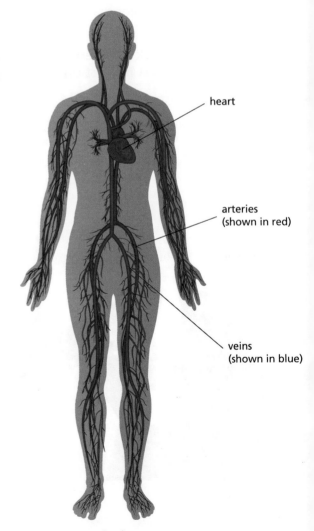

heart

arteries (shown in red)

veins (shown in blue)

FIG 2.6 Human circulatory system

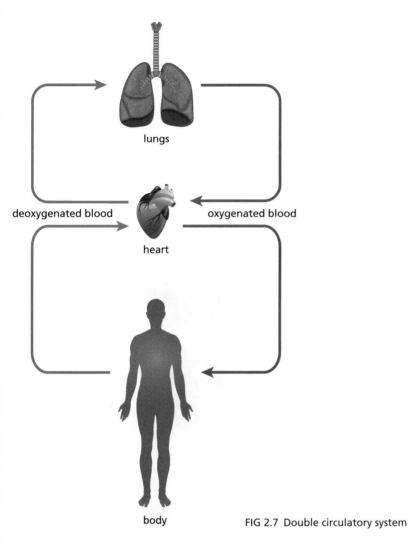

lungs

deoxygenated blood

oxygenated blood

heart

body

FIG 2.7 Double circulatory system

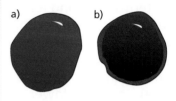
In the other circuit, blood passes between the heart and the rest of the body. Essential substances such as oxygen and glucose are carried to the cells of the body and waste products such as carbon dioxide and urea are removed.

This double system has the advantage that the blood to the rest of the body can be pumped by the heart at a much higher pressure than would otherwise be the case. This ensures that oxygenated blood reaches all parts of the body.

Check your understanding

1. Copy and complete the following sentences.

   a) Blood is pumped around the body by the
   _____ .

   b) Blood receives oxygen in the _____ .

2. What happens in the lungs?

3. What is the advantage of the double circulatory system?

Key terms

circulatory system
system that carries blood around the body

heart muscular four-part sack that is at the centre of the circulatory system and pumps blood around the body

double circulatory system a circulation system where one circuit is from the heart to the lungs and back, and the other is from the heart to the rest of the body and back

The heart

We are learning how to:

- relate the main parts of the circulatory system to its function in the human body
- describe how the heart works.

The heart ⟫⟫

The heart is a muscular organ that pumps blood around the body.

The heart has four chambers. The terms right and left are used as if you are viewing a person's heart from the front of their body. There are two upper chambers – **auricles (atria)** – and two lower chambers – **ventricles**.

The two sides of the heart are separated by a thick muscular wall – the **septum**. This prevents the **oxygenated** blood in the left side from mixing with the **deoxygenated** blood in the right side.

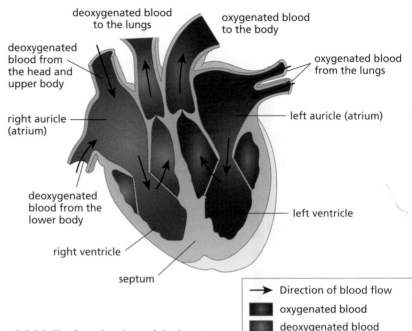

deoxygenated blood to the lungs

oxygenated blood to the body

deoxygenated blood from the head and upper body

oxygenated blood from the lungs

right auricle (atrium)

left auricle (atrium)

deoxygenated blood from the lower body

left ventricle

right ventricle

septum

→ Direction of blood flow

oxygenated blood

deoxygenated blood

FIG 2.9 The four chambers of the heart

The flow of blood through the heart is as follows:

body → right auricle → right ventricle → lungs → left auricle → left ventricle → body

Deoxygenated blood returns to the right auricle of the heart from all parts of the body. The blood passes into the right ventricle and is then pumped to the lungs, where it absorbs oxygen and releases carbon dioxide.

The oxygenated blood flows from the lungs into the left auricle. In the heart the blood passes into the left ventricle from where it is pumped to all parts of the body.

Diastole and systole

The heart continues to pump by repeatedly contracting and relaxing every second that you are alive. Heart muscle does not become exhausted and stop as other muscles might.

The moment when the heart muscle relaxes is called the **diastole**. During this time:

- deoxygenated blood from the body enters the right auricle
- oxygenated blood from the lungs enters the left auricle.

The moment when the heart muscle contracts is called the **systole**. During this time:

- the auricles contract, forcing blood into the ventricles
- when full, the ventricles contract, forcing blood out of the heart.

There are valves in the heart to make sure the blood only flows in one direction and cannot flow backwards.

Activity 2.2

Examining a goat's heart

Here is what you need:

- goat's heart
- scissors
- scalpel
- dissecting pins.

Here is what you should do:

1. Carefully examine the outside of the heart. Can you see the coronary blood vessels that supply the heart muscle with blood?
2. Observe where the blood vessels attached to the heart are connected.
3. Cut into the heart and identify the four chambers.
4. Look for the valves that prevent blood flowing backwards.

Check your understanding

1. **a)** In what order does blood pass through the chambers of the heart?

   b) Which chambers of the heart contain:

   i) oxygenated blood?

   ii) deoxygenated blood?

Medical fact

Some people are born with a congenital defect – a hole in their heart. This means that there is a hole in the septum. This allows deoxygenated blood to pass from the right side of the heart to the left side without passing through the lungs.

As a result, the person's blood does not carry sufficient oxygen around the body so they lack energy and are often tired. This condition can be corrected by surgery to seal the hole.

Key terms

auricles (atria) upper chambers of the heart

ventricles lower chambers of the heart

septum thick muscular wall that separates the two sides of the heart

oxygenated contains oxygen

deoxygenated does not contain oxygen

diastole the moment when the heart muscle relaxes

systole the moment when the heart muscle contracts

Arteries, veins and capillaries

We are learning how to:

- relate the main parts of the circulatory system to its function in the human body
- identify differences between arteries, veins and capillaries.

Arteries and veins ▶▶▶

Arteries	Veins
carry blood away from the heart	carry blood to the heart
most carry oxygenated blood (exception is pulmonary artery)	most carry deoxygenated blood (exception is pulmonary vein)
thick outer wall — narrow diameter — thick layer of muscles and elastic fibres — FIG 2.10 Cross-section through an artery	fairly thin outer wall — large diameter — thin layer of muscles and elastic fibres — FIG 2.11 Cross-section through a vein
have thick walls that include a thick layer of muscle to withstand high pressure of blood leaving heart	have thinner walls and contain less muscle as blood pressure inside vein is much less than in artery
inside diameter or **lumen** of an artery is relatively small	inside diameter or lumen is wider than that of an artery
the blood flow is at high pressure so valves are not needed as there is no chance of back flow	the blood flowing through veins does not have the benefit of high pressure created by the pumping heart. Instead, it relies on being squeezed through the veins as a result of muscle action. In order to prevent blood flowing backwards, long veins, such as those in the arms and legs, have valves that allow the blood to flow in one direction only.
artery arterioles FIG 2.12 Large arteries divide into smaller arterioles	open valve — wall of vein — vein squeezed by body muscle — if blood flows back, it fills the pockets, closing the valve — direction of blood flow → FIG 2.13 Long veins contain non-return valves

TABLE 2.1

Capillaries

Arteries and veins are ideal for transporting blood from one part of the body to another but their walls are far too thick for substances to diffuse into and out of them.

Arteries subdivide many times, first forming **arterioles** and finally a network of blood **capillaries** so that every cell is supplied with blood.

Blood capillaries are much thinner than human hair and their walls are only one cell thick. This allows substances such as oxygen and glucose to diffuse out into the cells while, at the same time, waste products such as carbon dioxide and urea diffuse out of the cells.

As the blood flows through the capillaries, it provides the substances that the cells require. The capillaries leaving the cells join together to form slightly larger blood vessels called **venules**, which then combine to become veins, carrying the blood back to the heart.

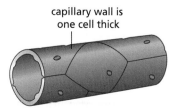

capillary wall is one cell thick

FIG 2.14 A blood capillary

Fun fact

The artery that connects the heart with the lungs is the only artery in the body that carries deoxygenated blood. It is called the pulmonary artery.

Activity 2.3

Cross-sections of blood vessels

Here is what you need:

- art paper
- paints or coloured pens/pencils.

Here is what you should do:

1. Draw a cross-section of an artery, a vein and a capillary next to each other.

2. Use a different colour for each of the materials in the blood vessel walls.

3. Label your blood vessels.

Check your understanding

1. Explain why:

   a) the walls of an artery need to be thicker than the walls of a vein

   b) long veins have valves but long arteries do not

   c) the walls of blood capillaries are much thinner than the walls of arteries or veins.

Key terms

arteries vessels that are part of the circulatory system that carries blood away from the heart

veins vessels that are part of the circulatory system that carries blood to the heart

lumen inside diameter of an artery or vein

arterioles subdivisions of arteries

capillaries vessels that are part of the circulatory system; they are very thin, have walls one cell thick and allow substances to diffuse out into cells

venules larger blood vessels formed by capillaries joining together

Components of the blood

We are learning how to:

- relate the main parts of the circulatory system to its function in the human body
- identify different components of blood.

Blood

Blood consists of a liquid part – plasma – and a solid part made up mostly of blood cells. Plasma is about 90 per cent water but also contains some important substances including:

- nutrients obtained by the digestion of food, which are being taken to the cells of the body

- waste products such as urea, which will eventually be excreted from the body

- blood proteins such as antibodies, which help to protect the body from disease, and fibrinogen, which helps the blood to clot

- hormones that coordinate different functions within the body.

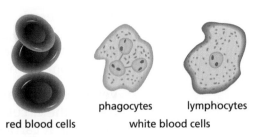

red blood cells	phagocytes	lymphocytes
	white blood cells	

FIG 2.15 Red and white blood cells

The mass of blood cells contains a mixture of both **red blood cells** and **white blood cells**, each with vital roles in our well-being. It also contains **platelets**. Platelets look like fragments of red blood cells. They are essential for the clotting process.

Activity 2.4

Observing blood cells

Here is what you need:

- microscope
- prepared slides showing different blood cells.

Here is what you should do:

1. Place the prepared slides under a microscope and observe first under low power and then under high power.

2. Draw examples of the blood cells you observe.

Red blood cells	White blood cells
• transport oxygen around the body • contain a pigment called haemoglobin, which contains iron • a shortage of red blood cells causes anaemia – a condition that may be due to insufficient iron in the diet	• fight any infection that might enter the body • there are two types, **phagocytes** and **lymphocytes**, which fight infection in different ways • phagocytes enclose bacteria or parts of bacteria into the cell and then digest them and kill them • lymphocytes release chemicals – antibodies – that destroy bacteria

TABLE 2.2

Check your understanding

1. Fig 2.16 shows a sample of blood viewed through a microscope.

Which of the following are indicated by A, B, C and D?

a) Platelets

b) Lymphocyte

c) Red blood cell

d) Phagocyte

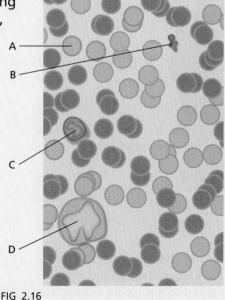

FIG 2.16

Fun fact

Every year thousands of people in Trinidad and Tobago donate blood to help others.

FIG 2.17

The blood is given to patients who have lost blood as a result of an accident or during surgery.

Key terms

red blood cells cells that transport oxygen around the body

white blood cells cells that fight any infection that might enter the body

platelets small blood particles that are essential for the clotting process

phagocytes cells that enclose bacteria or parts of bacteria into the cell and then digest them and kill them

lymphocytes cells that release chemicals called antibodies that destroy bacteria

Pulse rate

We are learning how to:

- investigate the relationship between exercise and pulse rate
- measure pulse rate.

The pulse ⟫⟫

Pulses of blood are the result of the heart contracting and relaxing. The **pulse rate** is the number of times this occurs in one minute.

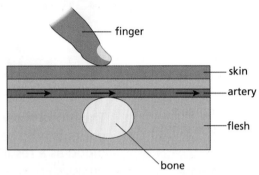

FIG 2.18 Feeling a pulse

Arteries are generally too deep in the flesh to feel the blood pulsing through them but at certain points in the body an artery passes over a bone just under the skin, for example at the wrist, neck, temple and ankle. This makes it possible to feel the pulsing of the blood.

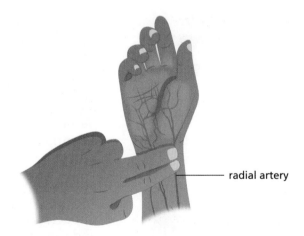

FIG 2.19 The radial pulse

The most commonly used point is inside the wrist about two centimetres under the thumb. This is sometimes called the **radial pulse** because it is the result of blood passing along the radial artery to the hand.

A child's pulse rate gradually decreases as they get older and stabilises around the age of ten. The pulse rate of a newborn baby can be as high as 190 beats per minute.

Stage of development	Pulse rate range in beats per minute
newborn to 1 month old	70–190
1 month to 1 year old	80–160
1–2 years old	80–130
3–4 years old	80–120
5–6 years old	75–115
7–9 years old	70–110
Over 10 years old	60–100

TABLE 2.3

An average adult has a pulse rate in the range 60–80 beats per minute. Notice that pulse rate is given as a range. This is because people are all a little bit different. An adult with a pulse rate of 60 beats per minute may be just as healthy as one who has a pulse rate of 80 beats per minute.

You should already be familiar with taking a pulse from the work in Form 1. Use Activity 2.5 to remind yourself how to take a pulse. You will need to remember how to do this for the next lesson.

Activity 2.5

Measuring your own pulse rate

Here is what you need:

- stopwatch.

Here is what you should do:

1. Search for the radial pulse on the inside of your wrist.

2. Place your fingers (not your thumb) on the inside of your wrist.

3. Count the number of pulses in one minute.

Check your understanding

1. What happens to the pulse rate as a person gets older?

2. Why can a pulse be felt at certain parts of the body?

Fun fact

FIG 2.20

A giraffe has a large powerful heart to pump blood up its long neck against the pull of gravity.

Key terms

pulse rate the number of times the heart contracts and relaxes in one minute

radial pulse the pulse inside the wrist just under the thumb

Effect of exercise on pulse rate

We are learning how to:

- investigate the relationship between exercise and pulse rate
- relate level of activity to pulse rate.

Exercise and pulse rate

The circulatory system supplies the body with oxygen and glucose, which are needed to generate energy.

When the body becomes more active, perhaps as a result of taking **exercise**, it will need more energy. You might therefore expect the pulse rate to increase as the heart works harder to keep up with demand.

FIG 2.21 Exercise needs energy

Activity 2.6

Investigating the effects of exercise on pulse rate

It is better to work with a partner for this activity.

Here is what you need:

- stopwatch.

Here is what you should do:

1. Sit at your desk and relax. While you are relaxing, draw a table in your book like Table 2.4.

2. When you and your partner are both relaxed, measure each other's pulse rates at rest.

3. You should both now take five minutes of gentle exercise, such as walking. Your teacher will tell you what to do.

4. After five minutes of gentle exercise, measure each other's pulse rate. Write these values in the table.

5. Your partner and you should now take five minutes of vigorous exercise, such as running. Your teacher will tell you what to do.

6. After five minutes of vigorous exercise, measure each other's pulse rate. Write these values in the table.

	When I am at rest	When I have taken gentle exercise	When I have taken vigorous exercise
number of pulses per minute			

TABLE 2.4

7. What is the effect of exercise on the pulse rate?

8. Represent the data you have gathered as a bar graph.

Pulse rate is also called **heart rate**. Runners and other athletes can check their heart rate as they exercise by wearing a **heart monitor**.

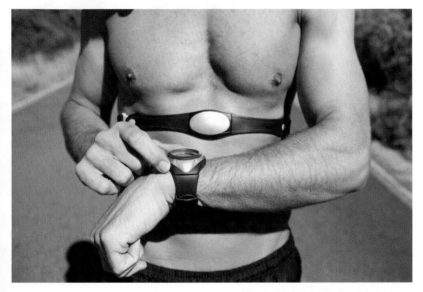

FIG 2.22 Heart rate monitor

FIG 2.23 Monitoring heart rate while you exercise

The heart monitor consists of two parts. One part is a band that fits around the chest and the other is a special watch on their wrist. The monitor is positioned over the heart so that it can detect each heartbeat. This information is sent to the wristwatch using a short-range radio signal.

The wristwatch shows the heart rate.

Key terms

exercise anything that raises heart rate

heart rate the number of times the heart beats per minute

heart monitor a device that detects heartbeats

Check your understanding

1. What is the effect of exercise on heart rate?

2. How does a heart monitor work?

Health and the circulatory system

We are learning how to:

- identify health conditions associated with the circulatory system
- explain things that have a detrimental effect on circulation.

Health and circulation »»

The circulatory system is essential to a person's health. If it ceases to function correctly this has a very profound effect on their lifestyle.

Atherosclerosis

Atherosclerosis is a condition in which fatty deposits – **plaque** – grow on the inside of arteries.

Scientists are not sure why plaque builds up in the arteries but the following factors increase the chances of having this condition:

- smoking
- a diet that contains a lot of fat
- being overweight or obese
- not taking regular exercise
- having high blood pressure or type 2 diabetes.

A person with atherosclerosis will lack energy because their cells are not receiving enough nutrients and oxygen. Treatment involves changing their lifestyle. When an artery becomes badly blocked, surgery may be required to bypass the blocked section.

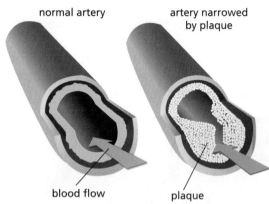

FIG 2.24 Plaque makes the artery narrower so that blood cannot flow through it as freely as it should

High blood pressure

Blood pressure is recorded as two figures, **systolic pressure** and **diastolic pressure**, and is measured in millimetres of mercury, mmHg. If your blood pressure is 110 over 75, you have a systolic pressure of 110 mmHg and a diastolic pressure of 75 mmHg. The instrument used to measure blood pressure is called a **sphygmomanometer**.

Normal blood pressure for an adult is 120 over 80. If a person's blood pressure is consistently 140 over 90 or greater, they have **high blood pressure (hypertension)**. Scientists do not know exactly why high blood pressure develops but the following factors increase a person's risk of high blood pressure:

- smoking
- being overweight

Fun fact

In heart bypass surgery, surgeons use sections of blood vessels from other parts of the body to bypass blocked coronary arteries.

- drinking too much alcohol
- drinking too many drinks containing caffeine
- not taking regular exercise
- eating too much salt with food.

People are also at higher risk if they are over 65 years old, have relatives with high blood pressure or are of African or Caribbean descent.

Taking regular exercise, eating a diet with less salt, or drinking less alcohol or fewer drinks containing caffeine can all help control high blood pressure.

Varicose veins

Varicose veins are swollen veins that occur mostly in the legs. They develop when the small valves in the veins stop working properly. Blood is able to flow backwards and collect in the vein causing it to swell.

Varicose veins are associated with old age and being overweight, and may also develop during pregnancy.

For most people, varicose veins do not affect their blood circulation but they have an unpleasant appearance. They can be treated with pressure stockings or, in severe cases, by surgery.

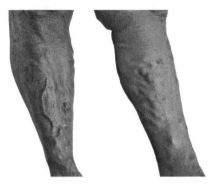

FIG 2.25 Varicose veins

Activity 2.7

Heath and the circulatory system

Here is what you should do:

1. Choose one of the circulatory problems discussed above.

2. Carry out some research to find out some more details.

3. Prepare a brief presentation to be given to the class. Make use of pictures, diagrams, a slideshow or video, to make your presentation as interesting as possible.

Check your understanding

1. **a)** What is considered to be normal blood pressure for an adult male?

   b) What is the significance of the two numbers quoted for blood pressure?

   c) A man is told by his doctor that he has high blood pressure. Suggest three ways the man might alter his lifestyle in order to lower it.

Key terms

atherosclerosis condition in which plaque grows on the inside of arteries

plaque fatty deposits that grow inside arteries

systolic pressure the blood pressure when the heart muscle contracts

diastolic pressure the blood pressure when the heart muscle relaxes

sphygmomanometer the instrument used to measure blood pressure

high blood pressure (hypertension) condition where blood pressure is higher than normal

varicose veins swollen and enlarged veins

Review of Human body systems: the circulatory system

- The circulatory system consists of the heart and a network of blood vessels that carry blood to all the cells of the body.

- The heart is a muscular sack that contracts and relaxes throughout a person's life without ever stopping. It consists of four chambers:
  - right auricle – receives deoxygenated blood from the body
  - right ventricle – pumps deoxygenated blood to the lungs
  - left auricle – receives oxygenated blood from the lungs
  - left ventricle – pumps oxygenated blood to the body.

- The diastole is the moment when the heart muscle relaxes. During this time:
  - deoxygenated blood from the body enters the right auricle
  - oxygenated blood from the lungs enters the left auricle.

- The systole is the moment when the heart muscle contracts. During this time:
  - the auricles contract, forcing blood into the ventricles
  - when full, the ventricles contract, forcing blood out of the heart.

- Blood is carried away from the heart in arteries and towards the heart in veins.

- Arteries have thick muscular walls and a small lumen. They must withstand very high pressures as blood is pumped into them from the heart.

- Veins have thinner walls and a larger lumen. The pressure in veins is less than in arteries. Long veins have valves to prevent blood flowing in the wrong direction.

- Arteries divide into arterioles and then into capillaries. The wall of a blood capillary is only one cell thick so substances are able to pass between capillaries and cells. Capillaries combine to form venules. Venules combine to form veins.

- Blood consists of about 90 per cent liquid, which is called plasma, and ten per cent solids, which is mostly blood cells.

- Plasma contains:
  - nutrients, such as glucose and amino acids
  - waste products, such as urea
  - blood proteins
  - hormones.

- There are different types of blood cells:
  - red blood cells that carry oxygen around the body
  - white blood cells that engulf germs – phagocytes
  - white blood cells that release chemicals that kill germs – lymphocytes.

- A pulse is caused by blood being pumped through arteries by the heart.

- A pulse can be felt at different points of the body where an artery passes over a bone near the surface of the skin. One of the easiest places to feel a pulse is the inside of the wrist.

- Pulse rate is the number of pulses per minute. Pulse rate increases during exercise as the body needs more glucose and oxygen to provide energy.

- Atherosclerosis is a problem of the circulatory system caused by deposits of plaque in arteries, making them narrower.

- Blood pressure is expressed as two numbers. The first is the systolic pressure, when the auricles and then ventricles contract. The second is diastolic pressure, when blood flows into the auricles.

- Normal adult blood pressure is 120 over 80. A person is considered to have high blood pressure if their readings are consistently 140 over 90 or greater.

- Varicose veins are caused by the failure of valves in the long veins, often in the legs. Blood is able to flow back in the veins and collects, causing the veins to swell.

Review questions on Human body systems: the circulatory system

1. **a)** Why is the human circulatory system described as a 'double' circulatory system?

   b) State three differences between an artery and a vein.

2. Fig 2.RQ.1 shows a section through a blood vessel.

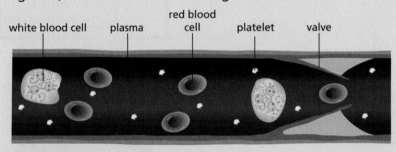

FIG 2.RQ.1

   a) Does Fig 2.RQ.1 represent an artery, a vein or a blood capillary? Explain your answer.

   b) In which direction does the blood flow through this vessel? Explain how you know.

3. Athletes eat a diet that is rich in carbohydrates to provide their bodies with lots of energy.

   a) Explain why athletes sometimes put on weight when they retire from athletics.

   b) Name one condition of the circulatory system that is more likely to occur in a person who is overweight.

   c) Explain what potential damage this condition might do to the circulatory system.

4. In Fig 2.RQ.2, X and Y represent two different types of blood vessel.

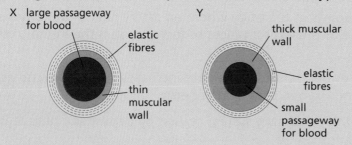

FIG 2.RQ.2

a) State whether each of these blood vessels is an artery, a vein or a capillary.

b) State whether each of the following statements is true or false.

   i)   All veins carry deoxygenated blood.

   ii) Arteries always carry blood away from the heart.

   iii) Capillaries have walls that are only one cell thick.

   iv) Arteries contain valves to prevent blood flowing in the wrong direction.

5. Fig 2.RQ.3 shows how the heart and lungs are connected.

a) Copy Fig 2.RQ.3 and draw arrows to show the direction of blood flow between the heart and the lungs and between the heart and the body.

b) Why does blood always flow in the same direction in:

   i) an artery?

   ii) a vein?

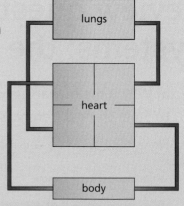

FIG 2.RQ.3

6. a) State two differences between the composition of the blood in the right ventricle and that in the left ventricle of the heart.

b) Fig 2.RQ.4 shows the heart of a 54-year-old man. A blockage has developed at X in one of the blood vessels.

   i) What is likely to be the effect of this blockage?

   ii) How could a heart bypass operation solve this problem?

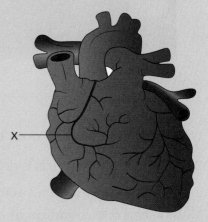

FIG 2.RQ.4

7. a) Explain why the blood pumped from the heart to the body is brighter red than the blood that returns to the heart.

b) Fig 2.RQ.5 says shows details of the human heart.

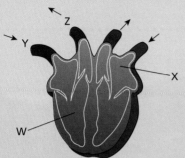

FIG 2.RQ.5

   i)   Identify the chambers of the heart marked W and X.
   ii) State where the blood comes from to Y.
   iii) State where the blood goes to from Z.

c) Some people are born with a hole between the two sides of their heart. Explain why this leaves them feeling weak and lacking in energy.

8. Jessica skipped for 15 minutes. When she stopped her pulse rate was taken for ten minutes. The results are given in Table 2.5.

Pulse rate (beats per minute)	113	100	88	79	73	69	66	64	63	62	62
Time (minutes)	0	1	2	3	4	5	6	7	8	9	10

TABLE 2.5

a) Draw a graph of pulse rate on the vertical axis against time on the horizontal axis.

b) Explain why skipping increases the pulse rate.

c) What is Jessica's pulse rate at rest?

Creating a 'Healthy Lifestyle' booklet

Scientists have long been aware that people who do not develop a healthy lifestyle at an early age often suffer for it later in life. Treating the problems created by a bad lifestyle, such as high blood pressure, diabetes and atherosclerosis is costly for regional health authorities as well as unpleasant for the individual.

Ministries of Education have produced information booklets in the past but they are concerned that these are not getting the message over to young people. The material is seen as 'establishment' and perhaps not taken as seriously as it should.

FIG 2.SIP.1 Active day at school

In a fresh approach, the Ministry in your country has decided to commission a 4-page booklet about developing a healthy lifestyle targeted at students between 11–16 years, written and designed entirely by students of that age group. As you have recently been studying the circulatory system, you have been hired by the Ministry to produce this booklet.

1 You are going to work in groups of 3 or 4 to produce an interesting, attractive and factually correct 4-page booklet on healthy lifestyle that will appeal to your own age group. The tasks are:

- To review the work on health and the circulatory system in the unit
- To research into aspects of a healthy lifestyle
- To identify several important areas that will be the focuses of your booklet
- To write the factual content of the booklet
- To consider the design of the booklet
- To produce a 'mock up' of the booklet for comment by reviewers
- To produce a completed booklet.

a) Look back through those parts of the unit that are concerned with health and the circulatory system. Make sure you are familiar with the different aspects which are covered and what is said about them.

b) Spend some time looking at factors which contribute to a healthy lifestyle. For example, you could find out about the role of a balanced diet and the importance of regular exercise.

You should avoid including long lists of 'dos' and 'don'ts' in your booklet as readers will not find this interesting.

c) You need to decide which aspects should be covered. You might decide, for example that regular exercise is very important because if it is not carried out the consequences can be very serious. Conversely, eating the odd chocolate bar may not be the best choice of food but you may consider it is less important.

d) Once you have decided which aspects of a healthy lifestyle are to feature in your booklet the next task is to write the text. Here are some issues for you to consider:

- You have limited space so comments need to be brief
- You are writing for students of mixed ability so use simple language that everyone can understand
- Pictures can often be used in place of text. You could take some pictures of other students in your group carrying out activities like exercising.

e) The design of your booklet is a key feature of this product. You want to stimulate peoples' interest enough to want to pick up your booklet and read it. How are you going to achieve this? Here are some ideas to think about:

- People are attracted by colours. You should consider how colour can be used for things like background tints, title boxes and text.
- Different font sizes can be used for titles, text and picture captions.
- Important messages can be emphasised using **bold**, *italic* or <u>underlined</u> text.
- Each page should have a similar balance of text and illustration.
- Pictures need to be big enough to see detail but not so big they dominate the booklet and people don't bother reading the text.

f) Make a 'mock up' of your booklet by folding a sheet of A4 paper in half. This will give you 4 pages. You can use white or coloured paper. If you decide on colour, light pastel shades are better for the background than intense colours.

You might find it useful to number the pages to avoid confusion later. You could start off by drawing a rough layout of how you envisage each page will look. This will give you an indication of how much room is available for text and what size your pictures should be. If you find there is too much text to fit the space available you will have to review what you have written.

You can give some thought as to whether you will use a colour tint to give your text boxes a coloured background. You also need to decide on font sizes and colours.

You can print out your text in suitably sized text boxes and alter the sizes of pictures before printing to ensure they will fit in the picture boxes. Cut out the printed text and pictures and stick them into your booklet.

Don't forget to save your text files and pictures so that if you decide to make alterations you will not have to start from the beginning again.

g) One you are happy with your first draft of the booklet, ask some reviewers to look through it and comment. You might ask them to look at particular aspects such as:

- Are there any typos (spelling mistakes, missing full stops etc.)?
- Is the text as clear as it can be?
- Are the pictures meaningful?
- Overall is the booklet attractive and interesting?

h) Once you get feedback from your reviewers you should make whatever changes are necessary to the text and the pictures and produce a final version of your booklet.

Unit 3: Human body systems: the respiratory system

Introduction ⟫

The respiratory system is responsible for providing the body with oxygen and removing the waste gas, carbon dioxide. These gases pass around the body in the circulatory system.

Structure of the respiratory system

Air is taken into the body through the nose and sometimes through the mouth. Both of these connect to the trachea, which carries air down into the lungs. You can see that a person is breathing because their chest moves up and down, even when they are asleep.

Exchanging gases

Oxygen gas forms about one fifth of the air around us. It is essential for life. Without oxygen you would die. Carbon dioxide is a waste gas produced by the body. This must be removed before it damages the body.

In the lungs these gases are exchanged. Oxygen passes from the air into the body, and carbon dioxide passes in the opposite direction.

Breathing

Breathing is one of those actions that your body does automatically without you having to think about it. You started breathing the moment you were born and you will continue to breathe until the moment you die.

Breathing, however, requires muscular action, which alters the shape and size of the thoracic cavity, which contains the lungs. The change in shape and size produces changes in the pressure inside the cavity compared to the external pressure of the atmosphere.

Cell respiration

The term 'respiration' is used to describe both the action of breathing in and out and the chemical process that takes place in the cells of the body to release energy.

These processes are linked in that breathing in and out is the way in which the body is able to supply and remove the gases associated with respiration in the cells.

Breathing rate

Your breathing rate is the number of times you breathe in and out each minute. As you get older your breathing rate tends to get slower.

FIG 3.1 Breathing rate increases when you are active

Since breathing is associated with providing the body with oxygen in order to produce energy, it is not surprising that breathing rate is linked to level of activity. You breathe more frequently when you are active than when you are at rest.

Smoking

People who smoke tobacco inhale a mixture of chemicals into their lungs.

FIG 3.2 Cigarette smoke is a cocktail of harmful substances

Some of these chemicals are harmful and damage the inside of the lungs. This reduces the efficiency of the lungs and might lead to life-threatening conditions such as emphysema or lung cancer.

Fun fact

Fish do not have lungs. They have gills that enable them to absorb oxygen dissolved in the water.

FIG 3.3 Whales breathe air

However, some of the animals that live in the sea have lungs and breathe air. Whales have to return to the surface every so often in order to breathe out and breathe in.

Structure of the respiratory system

We are learning how to:

- outline the basic structure of the respiratory system
- identify the different parts of the respiratory system.

The respiratory system »»

The respiratory system is concerned with breathing. Oxygen is needed by the body for respiration and during this process carbon dioxide is produced. These gases are exchanged in the **lungs**. Water vapour is also lost from the body in exhaled air.

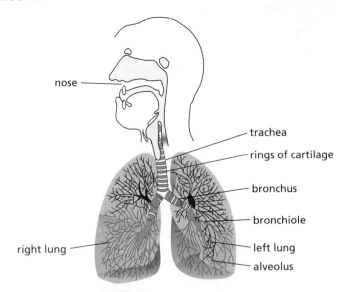

nose
trachea
rings of cartilage
bronchus
bronchiole
right lung
left lung
alveolus

FIG 3.4 Structure of the respiratory system

There are four parts to the respiratory system:

- the **nose,** where air is inhaled and exhaled
- the **trachea**, which carries air into and out of the chest
- the bronchi (singular **bronchus**), which connect the trachea to each of the lungs
- the two lungs, which are found on either side of the thoracic (chest) cavity, and are protected by the rib cage.

When you breathe in, air passes through the nose or mouth into the trachea. The trachea then divides into two bronchi, one serving each lung. Each bronchus divides many times to form smaller tubes called **bronchioles**. Each bronchiole ends in a collection of tiny air bags called **alveoli**.

Activity 3.1

Feeling the rings of cartilage in the trachea

You do not need any equipment or materials for this activity.

Here is what you should do:

1. Place your thumb pointing upwards on your throat just above your ribcage.

2. Gently push your thumb up and down your throat.

3. You should be able to feel some rings of cartilage. They are like the rings of wire inside the hose of a vacuum cleaner.

FIG 3.5

4. Cartilage is a stiff material that is more flexible than bone. Why do you think the trachea has rings of cartilage?

The capacity of the lungs increases as you grow up. The lung capacity of a young adult man is about 5.8 dm^3 while for a woman it is 4.2 dm^3. When you reach around 30 years old, the capacity starts to decrease.

When a person is 50 years old their lung capacity will only be about half of what it was in their youth. A reduced lung capacity means that less oxygen enters the body so less energy is obtained from respiration in the body cells. This explains why growing older is associated with shortage of breath and decreased endurance. Older people are also more susceptible to respiratory disorders.

Check your understanding

1. Arrange the following in the order that air passes through when you breathe in.

   alveolus bronchiole bronchus nose trachea

Fun fact

Pearl divers make regular dives into deep water to collect oysters in the hope that their shells will contain pearls.

FIG 3.6 Pearl divers

An experienced pearl diver can hold their breath for several minutes under water.

Key terms

lungs organs in body found on either side of the thoracic (chest) cavity and protected by the rib cage

nose where air is inhaled and exhaled

trachea carries air into and out of the chest

bronchus connects the trachea to a lung

bronchioles smaller tubes that connect to a bronchus

alveoli small air sacs found at the end of bronchioles

Gas exchange in the lungs

We are learning how to:

- outline the basic structure of the respiratory system
- explain the exchange of gases in the lungs.

Gas exchange ▶▶▶

Air is a mixture of gases. The main constituents are nitrogen (78%) and oxygen (21%). Air also contains a very small concentration (0.04%) of carbon dioxide.

When air enters an alveolus (one of the alveoli), these gases can pass through the alveoli walls and the walls of the blood capillaries that surround them.

Gases **diffuse** in both directions between the alveoli and the blood capillaries. The overall effect of **gaseous exchange** is determined by the relative **concentration** of each gas.

- **Oxygen** is in higher concentration in the alveoli as this is air that has just been inhaled. The concentration of oxygen in the blood is low as this is deoxygenated blood. So there will be a net movement of oxygen into the blood from the air.

- **Carbon dioxide** is produced by the body during respiration. Deoxygenated blood contains a much higher concentration of carbon dioxide than air. The result is a net movement of carbon dioxide from the blood into the air.

- Nitrogen diffuses into and out of blood in the same way as any other gas but, as it plays no part in cell respiration, the concentration in the blood remains the same. There is no net movement of nitrogen into or out of the blood.

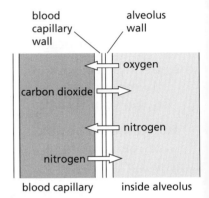

FIG 3.7 Diffusion of gases in the alveoli

Fun fact

The concentration of nitrogen dissolved in blood is not significant on land but it can affect a diver.

FIG 3.8

The deeper a diver goes, the more gas dissolves in their blood. If a diver rises to the surface too quickly, nitrogen gas will come out of solution and form bubbles at the joints. This condition is called 'the bends' and it is very painful.

Activity 3.2

To compare the concentration of carbon dioxide in inhaled and exhaled air

Here is what you need:

- two boiling tubes with bungs
- tubing
- T-piece
- limewater
- two stands and clamps.

Here is what you should do:

1. Set up the apparatus as shown in Fig 3.9. It is important that the tubes are the correct length and orientation.

2. Pour limewater into each boiling tube until it is about half full.

3. Slowly breathe in and out through the mouthpiece.

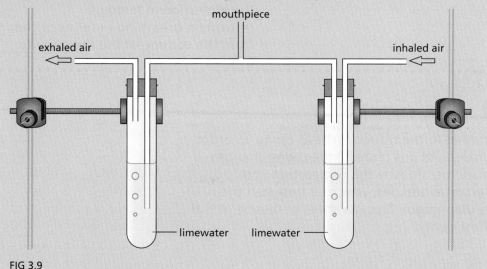

FIG 3.9

4. Limewater turns cloudy in the presence of carbon dioxide. In which boiling tube did the limewater turn cloudy first?

5. What can you deduce about the concentration of carbon dioxide in exhaled air compared to inhaled air?

Water is also produced during cell respiration. Much of this is lost through the lungs.

Exhaled air is always saturated in water vapour. If you breathe on a cold window or a mirror the water vapour condenses, forming a layer of tiny water droplets.

FIG 3.10 Water vapour condenses on a mirror

Check your understanding

1. Table 3.1 gives some information about the composition of inhaled and exhaled air.

	% of oxygen	% of carbon dioxide
inhaled air	21	0.04
exhaled air	16	4

TABLE 3.1

   a) What fraction of the oxygen in inhaled air is absorbed into the body?

   b) By how much is the concentration of carbon dioxide in exhaled air greater than the concentration in inhaled air?

Key terms

diffuse when gases move between two places

gaseous exchange exchange of gases from one place to another

concentration amount of gas present in a particular volume (of air)

oxygen a gas taken into the cells for respiration

carbon dioxide a gas produced by the body during respiration

How you breathe

We are learning how to:

- distinguish between breathing and respiration in humans
- explain breathing in terms of changes in the volume of the chest cavity.

Breathing ⟫

The lungs are situated in the thoracic (chest) cavity. In order to breathe in (**inhale**) and out (**exhale**) the cavity changes volume. This is made possible by the contraction and relaxation of **intercostal muscles**, which lie between the ribs, and also the **diaphragm**. This is a sheet of muscle at the bottom of the chest cavity.

Inhaling

When the intercostal muscles contract, they lift the ribs upwards and outwards. At the same time the diaphragm contracts and flattens. The result of this is that the volume of the chest cavity increases. The pressure of air decreases. The air pressure in the lungs is now less than atmospheric pressure so air is forced in to the lungs through the trachea.

The trachea has rings of cartilage along its length. These prevent the trachea from collapsing when the pressure in the lungs falls, or it would be impossible for air to enter the lungs.

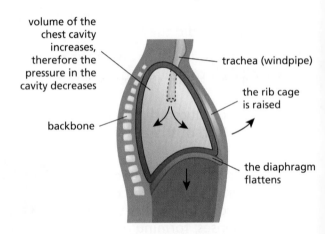

volume of the chest cavity increases, therefore the pressure in the cavity decreases

trachea (windpipe)

the rib cage is raised

backbone

the diaphragm flattens

FIG 3.11 Inhaling

Exhaling

This is the opposite process to inhaling.

The intercostal muscles contract, allowing the ribs to drop downwards and inwards. At the same time, the diaphragm muscle relaxes and it curves upwards. The result is a reduction in the volume of the chest cavity. The air pressure in the cavity is now greater than atmospheric pressure so air is forced out of the lungs through the trachea.

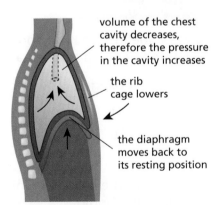

volume of the chest cavity decreases, therefore the pressure in the cavity increases

the rib cage lowers

the diaphragm moves back to its resting position

FIG 3.12 Exhaling

Activity 3.3

Breathing in and out

Your teacher will lead this activity.

Here is what you need:

- bell jar and bung
- rubber sheet
- Y-tube
- two balloons
- elastic band.

Here is what you should do:

1. Connect balloons to the two forks of a Y-tube using elastic bands.

2. Place the end of the Y-tube through a bung in the bell jar from the inside.

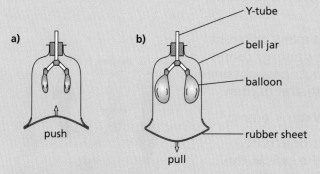

FIG 3.13

3. Draw a rubber sheet over the bottom of the bell jar and hold it in place with elastic bands.

4. Push the rubber sheet upwards as in Fig 3.13(a) and observe any change in the size of the balloons.

5. Pull the rubber sheet downwards as in Fig 3.13(b) and observe any change in the size of the balloons.

Check your understanding

1. **a)** Draw a table to show how the volume of the chest cavity and the pressure inside it change as a person breathes in and out.

   b) Name the muscles that contract and relax:

   i) between the ribs

   ii) at the bottom of the rib cage.

Medical fact

When a person is unable to breathe properly, perhaps as a result of an accident or surgery, a doctor can connect them to a ventilator.

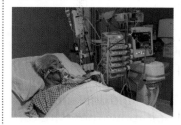

FIG 3.14

This is a machine that breathes for the person until their body has recovered.

Key terms

inhale breathe in

exhale breathe out

intercostal muscles muscles that lie between the ribs

diaphragm a sheet of muscle at the bottom of the chest cavity

Respiration in cells

We are learning how to:

- distinguish between breathing and respiration in humans
- describe the process of respiration that takes place in the cells of the body.

Respiration »»

The term 'respiration' can be misleading because in science it is used in two different ways.

- Respiration can be used to describe breathing in and out, and the exchange of gases in the lungs. To avoid confusion, this can be referred to as breathing.

- Respiration is also used to describe the process by which energy is released in cells by the reaction between food and oxygen. To avoid confusion, this process is known as **internal**, **cell** or **tissue respiration**.

All body cells require energy to power the many different chemical processes that go on in them. This energy comes from the chemical reaction between the nutrients obtained from the digestion of food, such as glucose and oxygen.

food + oxygen → carbon dioxide + water + energy

Carbon dioxide and water are the waste products of respiration. These are carried away from the cells in the blood. Respiration produces the carbon dioxide that is expelled from the lungs. Excess water is lost from the body by breathing, sweating and as urine.

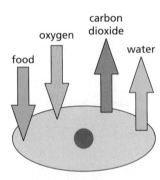

FIG 3.15 Respiration in a cell

Activity 3.4

Making a model of a cell

Make a model cell and use it to show how substances move into and out of the cell.

Here is what you need:

- materials for making a model, for example plastic bottles, small balls
- tools for cutting and shaping, for example scissors, craft knife.

Here is what you should do:

1. Build a model of a simple cell to show the nucleus and cytoplasm.
2. Show the movement of substances into and out of the cell in some way.

Within the cytoplasm of all cells – plant and animal – there are structures called mitochondria (singular **mitochondrion**).

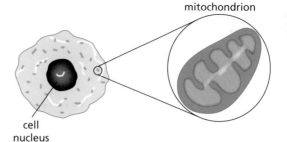

Mitochondria are sometimes called the 'powerhouses' of the cell because it is here that cell respiration takes place.

FIG 3.16 Mitochondria are in animal and plant cells

The concentration of mitochondria in different cells varies. Cells that require a continuous supply of energy have the highest concentration of mitochondria.

Heart muscle continually contracts and relaxes throughout our lives without a rest. Heart cells have a high concentration of mitochondria.

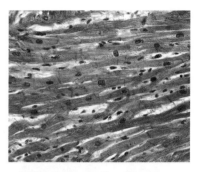

FIG 3.17 Heart muscle cells

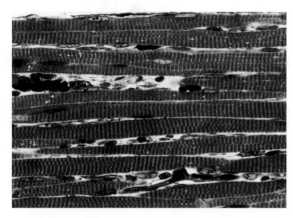

FIG 3.18 Skeletal muscle cells

Skeletal muscle is sometimes called voluntary muscle as it only contracts and relaxes when you decide to move. It requires less energy. These cells have a lower concentration of mitochondria than heart muscle cells.

Fun fact

Mitochondria vary in size and in number from one to over a thousand per cell. However, all mitochondria have the same basic structure.

Key terms

internal (cell/tissue) respiration the process by which energy is released in cells due to the reaction between food and oxygen

mitochondrion structure in cell where cell respiration takes place

Check your understanding

1. This equation represents the combustion of a fuel such as natural gas:

   fuel + oxygen → carbon dioxide + water + energy

   a) In what ways is this reaction similar to cell respiration?

   b) In what ways is this reaction different from cell respiration?

Breathing rate

We are learning how to:

- distinguish between breathing and respiration in humans
- measure breathing rate.

Breathing rate ⟫

Your **breathing rate** is how many times you breathe in and out each minute.

FIG 3.19 Breathing rate is low when you are relaxed or when you are asleep

FIG 3.20 Breathing rate increases when you are more active

Activity 3.5

Measuring breathing rate

If possible, work with a partner for this activity.

When somebody knows their breathing rate is being measured they become self-conscious and breathe more quickly. A doctor measures the breathing rate of a patient by observing them without the patient realising what is happening.

Here is what you need:

- stopwatch.

Here is what you should do:

1. Sit opposite your partner so you can watch each other.

2. Over a period of ten minutes, time the breathing rate of your partner five times but do not tell them when you are doing it.

3. Start timing and then count how many breaths they take in one minute.

4. Write down the number in a table like the one here.

	1st time	2nd time	3rd time	4th time	5th time
number of breaths in one minute					

TABLE 3.2

5. What was your partner's average breathing rate?

Breathing rate changes with age.

Age in years	Number of breaths per minute
Up to 1	30–60
1–3	24–40
3–6	22–34
6–12	18–30
12–18+	12–20

TABLE 3.3

As you grow older, the number of breaths you take each minute decreases. Breathing rate is always given as a range because people are all built a little bit differently.

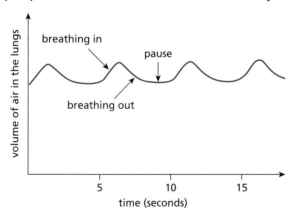

FIG 3.21 A typical pattern for breathing rate for a person at rest – each cycle of breathing in and breathing out is followed by a brief pause

Check your understanding

1. a) Estimate the breathing rate of the person in Fig 3.21 from the information given.

b) If Fig 3.21 represents the breathing rate at rest, suggest what age group the person belongs to.

Fun fact

People who feel under stress, often breathe less deeply and more often than normal. They can reduce the effects of stress and promote relaxation by controlling their breathing. This involves slowing the breathing rate and, at the same time, breathing more deeply.

Key term

breathing rate how many times you breathe in and out each minute

Exercise and breathing rate

We are learning how to:

- distinguish between breathing and respiration in humans
- explain why exercise affects breathing rate.

Effect of exercise on breathing rate ⟩⟩⟩

Oxygen is needed by the body to make energy in the body. The only way the body can obtain oxygen is by breathing.

FIG 3.22 When the body is at rest, normal breathing provides enough oxygen for the small amount of energy needed

FIG 3.23 When you exercise you must breathe more often and more deeply to get the extra oxygen needed to provide more energy

Activity 3.6

Measuring breathing rate after mild and strenuous exercise

Here is what you need:

- stopwatch.

Here is what you should do:

1. Look back to Activity 3.5 and copy your average breathing rate into a table like Table 3.4. This breathing rate was taken when you were at rest.

2. You and your partner should now take five minutes of gentle exercise, such as walking. Your teacher will tell you what to do.

3. After five minutes of gentle exercise, measure each other's breathing rate. Write this value in the table.

4. You and your partner should now take five minutes of vigorous exercise, such as running. Your teacher will tell you what to do.

5. After five minutes of vigorous exercise, measure each other's breathing rate. Write this value in the table.

	When I am at rest	When I have taken gentle exercise	When I have taken vigorous exercise
number of breaths per minute			

TABLE 3.4

6. What is the effect of exercise on the breathing rate?

If a person takes strenuous exercise, such as an athlete running very quickly, even rapid breathing cannot supply the body with enough oxygen for respiration. The body becomes short of oxygen. A period of recovery is required after exercise.

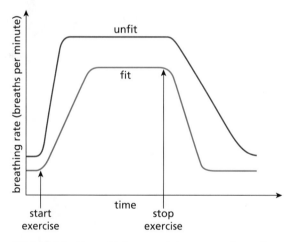

FIG 3.24 The time a person needs to recover depends on how fit their body is (the more fit they are the quicker they will recover and breathe normally again)

Check your understanding

1. a) What happens to a person's breathing rate when they exercise?

   b) Explain why it does this.

Fun fact

When a person exercises they may get a build-up of a substance called lactic acid in their muscles. The build-up of lactic acid causes pain in the muscles (a stitch). After they have finished exercising their body needs oxygen to break down the lactic acid. The amount of oxygen needed to do this is called the oxygen debt. This is why people carry on breathing hard even after they have finished exercising.

The effects of smoking

We are learning how to:

- relate increase in physical activity to increase in breathing rate
- relate smoking to damage of the respiratory system.

Smoking »»

Doctors know that there is a link between cigarette smoking and lung cancer. Smoking cigarettes does not always result in lung cancer, but a smoker has a very much greater chance of developing lung cancer than a non-smoker.

Cancer

Cancers are due to a rapid growth of tissue. Cancerous growths can occur in the lungs and in other organs.

When a doctor detects a cancerous growth in its early stages, there is a good chance it can be removed and the patient will survive. However, once a cancer is established in one organ, secondary cancers can appear in other organs and soon the patient is in a critical state.

Lung cancer is only one of several lung conditions that can be attributed to cigarette smoking.

Nicotine increases the heart rate and blood pressure. It is very addictive, which is why people find it difficult to stop smoking.

Carbon monoxide is a poisonous gas that bonds with haemoglobin in red blood cells. This prevents oxygen binding and so reduces the supply of oxygen to the cells of the body.

Tar is a mixture of many chemical Some of these are carcinogenic – they may cause cancers to grow.

FIG 3.25 The effects of three harmful substances produced when cigarettes are smoked

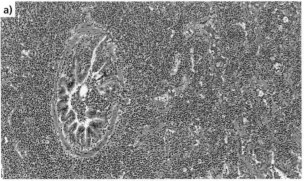
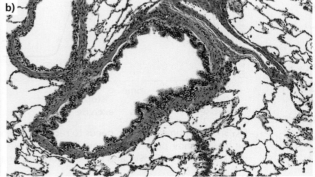

FIG 3.26 Normal and cancerous lung tissue: **a)** Cancerous lung tissue with many small cells filling the alveoli and bronchioles **b)** Normal healthy lung tissue with plenty of space for air to circulate through the alveoli and bronchioles

Circulation problems

Smoking also causes damage to the circulation.

Cigarette smokers are much more likely to suffer from **cardiovascular disease** (CVD), which can cause heart attacks and strokes.

Some chemicals in cigarette smoke enter the blood and cause fat to be deposited on the inside of arteries. These fatty deposits are called plaque.

Over time, less and less blood is able to reach the extremities of the body, such as the feet. This means that the cells in these parts of the body are not receiving sufficient nutrients or oxygen. The person may suffer partial or even total loss of use of these parts of the body, and they may need to be amputated.

Activity 3.7

The risks of smoking

Carry out some research.

Here is what you should do:

1. Use the information in the lesson and other sources to find out more about the effects that smoking has on the body in the short term and the long term.

2. Design and make a pamphlet advising young people about the risks of smoking.

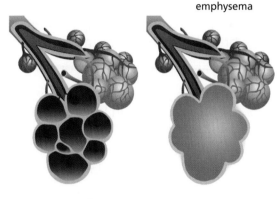

emphysema

normal

FIG 3.27 Emphysema is a disease that damages the structure of the alveoli

Emphysema

Smoking is a major cause of **emphysema**.

In normal lungs, the alveoli are like bunches of grapes. In emphysema, the inner walls break down, leaving one large air sac instead of many small ones.

The surface area across which gases can be exchanged is reduced and so less oxygen gets into the blood stream. Also, much of the stale air is not expelled during exhalation and becomes trapped in the lungs.

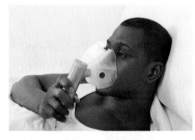

FIG 3.28 People with emphysema have difficulty absorbing sufficient oxygen for their body to behave normally. Chronic sufferers may even need to breathe in air that is enriched with oxygen

Fun fact

Nicotine is the addictive chemical present in tobacco smoke.

Some people are able to give up smoking by using nicotine patches, which they stick on their skin. The patches slowly release nicotine into the body so the person does not feel the need to smoke.

Key terms

cardiovascular disease disease associated with the circulatory system, which can cause heart attacks and strokes

emphysema condition in which the inner walls of alveoli break down, leaving one large air sac

Check your understanding

1. Name three harmful substances present in cigarette smoke.

2. Briefly describe how cigarette smoking can reduce the oxygen supply to the cells of the body.

3. Name the organs that are commonly affected by smoking.

Review of Human body systems: the respiratory system

- The respiratory system is the system of the body that is concerned with breathing.

- Air passes into the body through the nose and mouth and then through the trachea, bronchi, bronchioles and finally the alveoli in the lungs.

- The alveoli are air sacs found in clusters at the ends of the bronchioles.

- In the lungs, oxygen gas diffuses from the air, where it is in high concentration, into the blood, where it is in low concentration, through the alveoli walls and into the blood capillaries. At the same time, carbon dioxide diffuses out of the blood and into the air.

- Exhaled air contains a lower concentration of oxygen and a higher concentration of carbon dioxide than inhaled air.

- Inhalation and exhalation are brought about by the action of the intercostal muscles and the diaphragm. During inhalation, the volume of the chest cavity increases and therefore the pressure in the lungs becomes less than atmospheric pressure. Air is forced into the lungs. During exhalation, the volume of the chest cavity decreases and the pressure in the lungs becomes more than atmospheric pressure. Air is forced out of the lungs.

- Cell respiration is the process by which cells use nutrients from food and oxygen to provide energy.

  food + oxygen $\rightarrow$ carbon dioxide + water + energy

- Cell respiration takes place in structures called mitochondria, which are found in the cytoplasm of a cell. Heart muscle requires a lot of energy so heart muscle cells have a large number of mitochondria. Skeletal muscle needs less energy so skeletal muscle cells have fewer mitochondria.

- Breathing rate is the number of times a person breathes in and out each minute. The rate decreases as you grow to adulthood. A typical value for an adult male is between 12 and 20 breaths per minute.

- Breathing rate increases when the body exercises because it requires more oxygen for cells to produce more energy.

- The fitter a person is, the more quickly their body will recover after exercise and start breathing normally again.

- Smoking is responsible for an increased risk of a variety of illnesses and conditions, and a number of these are associated with the lungs. Cigarette smoke contains:

  o nicotine, which is an addictive drug

  o carbon monoxide, which combines with red blood cells and reduces the amount of oxygen being carried around the body

  o tar, which contains chemicals known to cause cancer.

- Tobacco smokers are at greater risk of developing lung cancer and other forms of cancer than non-smokers.

- Smoking tobacco also contributes to cardiovascular disease and other circulatory problems.

- Emphysema is a disease in which the walls of the alveoli break down and clumps of alveoli form single large air sacs. This greatly reduces the efficiency of the lungs so emphysema sufferers easily become short of breath.

Review questions on Human body systems: the respiratory system

1. Copy and complete the following sentences.

   a) When you breathe in your lungs fill with _____ .

   b) In the lungs _____ passes into the blood and _____ passes out.

   c) The body also loses excess _____ when you breathe out.

   d) The number of times a person breathes in and out each minute is called their _____ .

2. Fig 3.RQ.1 shows some parts of the body associated with respiration.
   a) Name the parts labelled A, B, C and D.

   b) Identify the other organ, shown in the chest cavity but not labelled.

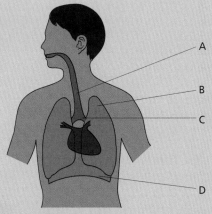

FIG 3.RQ.1

3. The apparatus in Fig 3.RQ.2 is used to investigate gaseous exchange during breathing.

   a) Limewater is used to test for which gas?

   b) What happens to the limewater if the gas is present?

   c) Which of the tubes in Fig 3.RQ.2 would show the presence of this gas first?

   d) What does the result of this investigation demonstrate?

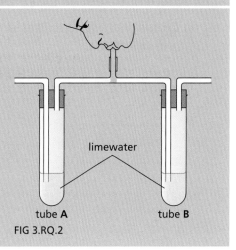

limewater

tube **A**   tube **B**

FIG 3.RQ.2

4. Amanda ran for five minutes. Fig 3.RQ.3 shows how her breathing rate changed after she stopped running and rested.

a) i) What was Amanda's breathing rate at the point when she stopped running?

ii) What is Amanda's normal breathing rate when she is at rest?

iii) How long did it take for Amanda's breathing rate to return to normal after she had stopped running?

b) Explain why running increases the breathing rate.

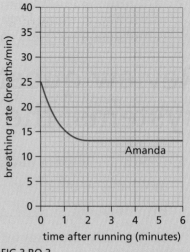

FIG 3.RQ.3

5. Fig 3.RQ.4 shows a model that can be used to demonstrate part of the mechanism for breathing.

a) Which parts of the respiratory system are represented by:

i) the bell jar?

ii) the glass tube?

iii) the balloons?

iv) the rubber sheet?

b) Explain why the volume of the balloons changes when the rubber sheet is moved up and down.

c) Suggest one reason why this is not a good model to show breathing.

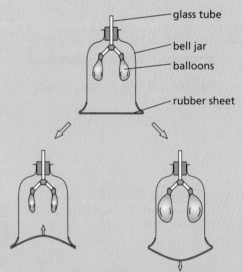

FIG 3.RQ.4

6. Electronic cigarettes (e-cigarettes) do not contain tobacco but a device that makes nicotine vapour.

a) Explain why e-cigarettes are safer than real cigarettes.

b) How might a person be able to use e-cigarettes to stop smoking tobacco?

FIG 3.RQ.5

7. Smoking tobacco is a cause of lung cancer. Table 3.5 gives some information about the number of deaths from lung cancer of men in the age range 40 to 80.

Group	Number of deaths per million men in the age range 40 to 80 years
cigar smokers	20
cigarette smokers	110
pipe smokers	30
mixed smokers who smoke two or more of the above	90
non-smokers	15

TABLE 3.5

Use the information in the table to answer these questions.

a) Display this information in the form of a bar graph.

b) What evidence is there that smoking tobacco is linked to lung cancer?

c) Which form of smoking carries the greatest risk?

d) Cigarette smokers who find it impossible to give up smoking are sometimes advised to switch from cigarettes to a pipe. Discuss whether this is good advice.

8. Table 3.6 gives some data on lung cancer.

Number of cigarettes smoked each day	0	10	20	30	40
Relative risk of lung cancer	1	17	31	55	82

TABLE 3.6

a) Show the data in the table as a line graph.

b) What does the graph indicate about smoking cigarettes and the risk of lung cancer?

c) Use your graph to estimate how much more likely a person smoking 35 cigarettes each day is to develop lung cancer than a person who does not smoke.

Unit 4: Physical and chemical processes

In this section, you will look at physical and chemical properties of matter, and types of mixtures.

Physical properties

Physical properties can be observed without changing the nature of the substance.

Some physical properties include:

- colour
- texture
- odour
- size
- melting point
- boiling point.

FIG 4.1 The colour, texture and density of gold are all physical properties

Chemical properties

When chemical changes occur, the nature of the substance involved undergoes changes where it may not be possible to identify the original substance.

FIG 4.2 Rusting is a chemical change

As substances undergo chemical changes, so their chemical properties change.

For example, hydrogen and oxygen are both highly reactive gases, but when they come together and undergo a chemical change to form water, the chemical properties of the product are different. Water is not so reactive. Its physical properties are also different in that it is a liquid at room temperature.

Chemical changes occur naturally all the time and include:

- food digestion
- cooking
- rusting
- fruit ripening.

FIG 4.3 Fruit ripening is a chemical change

Fun fact

Scientists claim that the energy from lightning storms on Saturn is enough to change methane into diamond. The atmosphere of Saturn contains methane. So while water droplets fall to Earth, diamonds rain on Saturn.

Physical properties of matter

We are learning how to:

- identify some observable physical properties of matter
- categorise properties into quantitative and qualitative.

Physical properties 〉〉〉

All matter has **physical properties** that are observable.

Activity 4.1

Observing properties

Here is what you need:

- materials such as sulfur, glass rod, stone, chalk, water, ice, wire, candle
- magnet
- batteries
- lamp
- nail
- connecting wire.

Here is what you should do:

Record your observations in a table like this.

Material	sulfur	glass	stone	chalk (etc.)
Colour				
Odour				
Does it conduct electricity?				
How hard is it?				
How elastic is it?				
Is the material attracted to a magnet?				

TABLE 4.1

1. Work first with the ice as it will melt quickly!
   Carefully examine each material and then carry out the following tests.

2. Build a circuit as shown below. Test for conductivity by putting each material into the circuit between the bulb and the battery to see whether the bulb lights up.

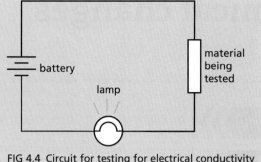

FIG 4.4 Circuit for testing for electrical conductivity

3. Test for hardness by scratching each material with a nail. The harder the material, the lighter the nail mark will be.

4. Stretch each material to test for elasticity.

The physical properties of a substance make it unique. These properties may be qualitative or quantitative.

Qualitative physical properties

Qualitative properties can be observed by using our five human senses, without changing the nature of the substance, for example:

- colour
- odour – the distinctive smell or aroma of the substance
- state – whether the substance is gaseous, liquid or solid.

Quantitative physical properties

Quantitative properties give numerical information with the use of measuring instruments, for example:

- electrical conductivity – the ability to allow electricity to flow through
- heat conductivity – the ability to transfer thermal energy
- solubility – the ability of a substance to dissolve in another
- melting point – the temperature at which the change from solid to liquid occurs
- boiling point – the temperature at which the change from liquid to gas occurs
- hardness – the ability to withstand scratches
- elasticity – the extent to which a material returns to its original shape after stretching
- magnetism – whether a material is attracted to a magnet.

Fun fact

The strength of 1 cm³ of human bone is five times that of concrete.

Key terms

physical properties related to the appearance of a material

qualitative properties can be described by words only

quantitative properties can be measured

Check your understanding

1. Which physical properties cannot be described fully using just your senses? How would you go about describing them more completely?

2. Give three examples of quantitative properties and three examples of qualitative properties.

Chemical changes

We are learning how to:

- identify some features of a chemical change.

Effervescence ›››

Activity 4.2

Observing a simple reaction (1)

Your teacher will drop some food colouring into solutions of an alkali, an acid and hydrogen peroxide, then cover and shake each.

1. Discuss your observations.

Activity 4.3

Observing a simple reaction (2)

You should work in groups of five or six.

Here is what you need:

- bottle
- dilute hydrochloric acid
- baking soda
- balloon
- spatula
- elastic band
- funnel.

Here is what you should do:

1. Using the funnel, place two spatulas of baking soda into the balloon.

2. Half fill the bottle with dilute hydrochloric acid. Do not spill any.

3. Without allowing the baking soda to fall into the acid, stretch the opening of the balloon to fit the mouth of the bottle and seal with the elastic band.

4. Place the bottle on the table and stand away.

5. Lift the flopping end of the balloon so that the baking soda is poured into the bottle. What do you observe?

6. What type of material is baking soda? What happened when it combined with an acid? What could happen if you shook the combination?

FIG 4.5 A chemical change causes the balloon to inflate

Hydrochloric acid is an **acid** and baking soda is a **base**. The two react together and fizzing occurs as a gas is produced. The gas caused the balloon to inflate in Activity 4.3. The production of gases, or **effervescence**, indicates a chemical reaction. Shaking might cause the balloon to burst.

Activity 4.4

Observing a simple reaction (3)

You should work in small groups.

Here is what you need:

- yeast
- hydrogen peroxide
- stirring rod
- thermometer
- test tube
- gloves.

SAFETY

Hydrogen peroxide is an irritant and a strong bleaching agent. Handle carefully. Reaction may be hot. Use gloves.

Here is what you should do:

1. Pour the hydrogen peroxide into the test tube, place the thermometer in and record its temperature.

2. Pour in the yeast and stir. What do you observe as the two substances combine?

3. What do you observe about the thermometer?

4. How does the outside of the test tube feel?

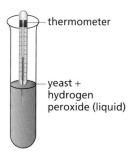

FIG 4.6 Measuring the temperature of yeast and hydrogen peroxide

When hydrogen peroxide reacts with yeast, both fizzing and heat are produced. Heat also indicates a **chemical change**.

Colour change

Alkali, acid and hydrogen peroxide react differently with food colouring. The colour change indicates a chemical change.

Check your understanding

1. What is observed when an acid reacts with baking soda?

2. What happens when yeast and hydrogen peroxide combine?

3. Chemical properties describe how a substance behaves when combined with another substance. Do you think chemical properties can be observed via our senses?

Fun fact

Chemicals can be used to give some foods distinctive flavours.

Key terms

acid a substance that will react with a base

base a substance that will react with an acid

effervescence the fizzing that occurs when an acid reacts with a substance to form a gas

chemical change a change that occurs when substances react together to form another substance

Comparing physical and chemical changes (1)

We are learning how to:

- classify changes as physical or chemical
- identify some differences between a physical and a chemical change.

The effect of heat on substances ⟫

Different substances behave differently when heated.

Activity 4.5

Heating substances

Here is what you need:

- salt
- soil
- lipstick
- candle
- brown or white sugar
- tin lids
- tongs
- matches
- tripod
- gauze
- Bunsen burner
- eye protection.

 SAFETY
Wear eye protection goggles for heating. Use correct procedure to light Bunsen burner. Do not touch hot apparatus and materials with bare hands.

Here is what you should do:

1. Place each material individually on a tin lid and heat over a *gentle* flame for no longer than two minutes. Note your observations.

2. Allow each substance to cool, then observe again.

3. Discuss your observations in your group.

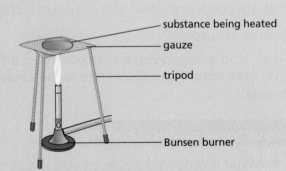
FIG 4.7 Apparatus for heating substances

You will have found that heating had little effect on salt and soil; the lipstick and the candle melted; and the sugar burned. The lipstick and the candle returned to the original substance on cooling. The sugar first melted and then it burned; it did not return to its original substance.

When a substance undergoes a change but can then return to the same substance with the same physical properties, it has undergone a physical change. This type of change is a **reversible change**.

When a substance undergoes a change and *cannot* return to the same substance with the same physical properties, it has undergone a chemical change. In all chemical changes, new products are formed. This type of change is usually an **irreversible change**.

Melting is a physical change. Burning is a chemical change. The fact that sugar burns is a chemical property of sugar.

> **Fun fact**
>
> While carbon is a black powder and hydrogen and oxygen are colourless gases, we all enjoy their chemical combination as sugar.

Activity 4.6

Writing a laboratory report for heating substances

Complete your laboratory report with the help of the following questions.

1. What was the aim of your experiment?

2. What apparatus and materials did you use?

3. How did you carry out the process of heating the materials? Draw a labelled diagram.

4. What safety precautions did you take?

5. How did you ensure your results were as accurate as possible? (For example, placing each substance on a clean lid and giving each substance the same heat intensity for the same time.)

6. What observations did you make? Did all the materials behave in the same way?

7. What conclusions can you draw from the experiment?

Check your understanding

1 From your experiment, two statements regarding the physical and chemical changes observed could be made. Copy and complete the following table. Allow space to add further rows to your table later.

	Physical change	Chemical change
1	The change ... be easily reversed.	The change ... be easily reversed.
2	No new substance is formed.	A new substance is formed.

TABLE 4.2

2 Melting is a physical change: it can be reversed. From your knowledge of changes of state, name some other reversible changes.

Key terms

reversible change
change where substance can go back to its original form

irreversible change
change where substance cannot go back to its original form

Comparing physical and chemical changes (2)

We are learning how to:

- identify more differences between physical and chemical changes.

Differences between physical and chemical changes

In the last experiment, you identified some differences between physical and chemical changes. In this experiment, you will identify further differences.

Activity 4.7

Comparing physical and chemical changes

Watch as your teacher demonstrates using aluminium and copper oxide.

Here is what you should do:

1. Observe each material. Describe its appearance.

2. Can you still identify each material when your teacher mixes them together? Would you be able to separate them?

3. Your teacher will then heat a small metal bowl of this mixture in a fume cupboard. Observe for a few minutes.

4. Can you explain what you observe?

5. Afterwards, look at the product and describe it. Could you recover the original substances?

FIG 4.8 Reacting aluminium and copper oxide: **a)** Aluminium filings **b)** Black copper oxide powder **c)** The results of the reaction between aluminium and copper oxide

Aluminium is a silvery metal and copper oxide is a black powder. When the two substances were mixed, it was possible to identify and separate each one because of their colour and particle size.

When the two substances were heated, the appearance of the bright firework explosions indicated that a chemical change had occurred. The individual properties of the substances were lost. The heat caused a **chemical reaction** between the aluminium and the copper oxide. New substances – aluminium oxide and copper metal – with new properties were formed. The reaction is represented by the equation:

aluminium + copper oxide $\rightarrow$ aluminium oxide + copper

$$2Al + 3CuO \rightarrow Al_2O_3 + 3Cu$$

Check your understanding

1 You can now make further statements regarding physical and chemical changes. Add rows to the table you started in the last lesson, as below, and complete it.

	Physical change	Chemical change
1	The change can be easily reversed.	The change cannot be easily reversed.
2	No new substance is formed.	A new substance is formed.
		The new substance formed has … properties.
3	When substances are mixed the components … be easily identified.	When substances are combined the components … be easily identified.
4	After substances are combined the original components … be easily separated.	After substances are combined the original components … exist.

TABLE 4.3

Fun fact

Gallium is an unusual metal that does not occur as a pure element in nature. A very interesting phenomenon about gallium is that it can melt in the palm of your hand.

Key term

chemical reaction
a reaction that takes place between two substances so that they combine to form a new substance or substances

Chemical reaction

We are learning how to:

- explain the changes occurring in a chemical reaction.

Changes in a chemical reaction ⟩⟩

Activity 4.8

Burning magnesium

You will now view another chemical reaction caused by heating. Your teacher will demonstrate this.

 SAFETY

Wear eye protection. Do not look directly at the magnesium ribbon as it is being burned.

Here is what you should do:

1. Observe the physical properties of magnesium ribbon.

2. Observe the magnesium while it is being heated over a flame.

3. Observe and discuss the results after heating.

4. What caused the formation of the powder?

5. The magnesium reacted with a gas in the air. Can you suggest which gas might give rise to such a bright flame?

  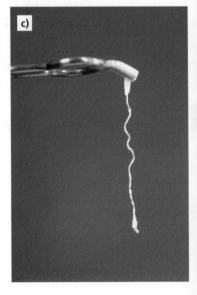

FIG 4.9 **a)** Magnesium ribbon **b)** Magnesium being heated **c)** Magnesium oxide

Magnesium ribbon is a thin strip of silver coloured metal. When the ribbon was heated, an extremely bright flame was produced. This flame was so bright that it could be harmful to look at directly. The burning indicated that a new substance was being formed.

The atoms of oxygen in the air fused (joined) with the atoms of magnesium. After the flame went out, the result was a white powder called magnesium oxide. This chemical reaction is:

magnesium + oxygen → magnesium oxide

$$2Mg + O_2 \rightarrow 2MgO$$

The Mg (magnesium metal) and the O_2 (oxygen gas) on the left of the **chemical equation** are the **reactants**. The heat causes them to react together. The MgO (magnesium oxide powder) on the right is the **product** of the reaction. It is a chemical combination of magnesium and oxygen atoms – they are bonded together to form a magnesium oxide **molecule**.

Key terms

chemical equation an equation that shows what happens during a chemical reaction

reactants the substances that react together in a chemical reaction

product a substance formed as a result of a chemical reaction

molecule the smallest particle of a chemical compound

FIG 4.10 Early photographers used burning magnesium as a light source for flash photography

Check your understanding

1. Explain the reaction between magnesium and oxygen.

Types of chemical reaction

We are learning how to:

- describe some different types of chemical reaction.

Combustion

Activity 4.9

Burning candle

Here is what you need:

- short piece of candle
- large beaker
- lid
- matches.

 SAFETY

Wear eye protection goggles for heating. Do not touch hot apparatus and materials with bare hands.

Here is what you should do:

1. Place the candle in the beaker and set it alight.

2. While it is still alight, place the lid over the beaker.

3. Does the candle remain lit? Why?

Combustion, also known as burning, is a chemical change. It begins with a spark. As long as that spark is 'fed', combustion will continue.

The components necessary for a fire are shown in the fire triangle. If any one component is removed, the flame will die down and combustion will cease. For example, in Activity 4.9 you placed the lid over the beaker, which cut off the supply of oxygen so the reaction stopped.

FIG 4.11 This is the 'Fire Triangle', which shows that combustion needs oxygen, fuel and heat

Decomposition

Activity 4.10

Observing a decomposition

Your teacher will demonstrate an experiment with hydrogen peroxide. From its name, what atoms do you think hydrogen peroxide is composed of? Observe as hydrogen peroxide is poured through the funnel and into manganese dioxide.

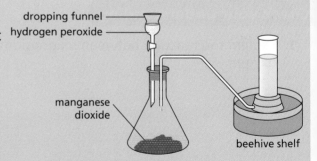

FIG 4.12 Apparatus for the decomposition of hydrogen peroxide

Here is what you should do:

1. Explain what your observations indicate.

2. Can you suggest which gas is produced?

3. If a glowing splint is placed in the gas, what do you think will happen to the glow?

A hydrogen peroxide molecule is composed of two atoms of hydrogen and two of oxygen. When it is poured onto manganese dioxide, it 'decomposes' very quickly into water and a gas. A gas test identifies the gas to be oxygen – since oxygen is the only gas that can set a glowing splint ablaze. This **decomposition** is a chemical change represented by the chemical equation:

hydrogen peroxide → water + oxygen

Chemical changes and heat

While some reactions give out heat, others take in heat.

> **Fun fact**
>
> The salt that you put on your food can be made by a chemical reaction between a highly reactive metal, sodium, and chlorine, a green poisonous gas. However, salt also occurs naturally.

4.7

Activity 4.11

Mixing sodium carbonate and dilute ethanoic acid

Here is what you need:

- beaker containing dilute ethanoic acid
- thermometer
- sodium carbonate
- spatula.

Here is what you should do:

1. Place the thermometer in the beaker of acid, record the temperature and feel the outside of the beaker.

FIG 4.13 Adding sodium carbonate to dilute ethanoic acid

2. Stir one spatula of sodium carbonate into the acid and observe the thermometer.

3. Feel the outside of the beaker and explain your observations.

In this reaction, the endothermic reaction causes the reaction vessel to cool and it takes in heat energy from the surrounding air.

Check your understanding

1. What was the fuel when each of the following burned?

   a) Paper   **b)** A match   **c)** A candle

2. What does a fuel react with in a combustion reaction?

3. Explain the similarities and differences between putting a beaker of ethanoic acid in the refrigerator and mixing it with sodium carbonate. Use these words: chemical, physical, reversible, irreversible.

Key terms

combustion a chemical change in which a fuel reacts with oxygen

decomposition a chemical change in which a substance breaks down into two or more substances

Everyday chemical changes

We are learning how to:

• observe chemical changes.

Chemical changes all around you ≫

Chemical changes take place around you all the time. Examples of this are combustion (burning), cooking, food digestion, the **rusting** of iron, **explosions**, **limescale** build-up, the cleaning actions of detergents, the ripening of fruit and food 'going off'.

Activity 4.12

Observing rust

Here is what you need:

• new nail
• rusted nail.

Here is what you should do:

FIG 4.14 Rusting of an iron nail

1. Look at the new nail and the old rusted nail.

2. Explain what has happened to the old one.

> **Fun fact**
>
> Nails are actually usually made from mild steel to give them greater strength. However, as this is mostly iron we can use them in experiments in place of iron.

Nails are made mostly of iron. Rusting occurs when oxygen in the air combines chemically with the iron. The iron oxide is brown and powdery.

iron (element) + oxygen (element) → iron oxide (compound)

FIG 4.15 Rusty iron bridges such as this will have to be replaced

Why you need chemical changes

All biological processes rely on chemical reactions. Here are some examples:

- digestion
- respiration
- fermentation
- photosynthesis
- rotting and recycling of nutrients.

In other words, life depends on chemical reactions.

When do you not need chemical changes

Iron is a very strong metal. It is used for structures such as bridges. When it rusts, some of the iron is changed to iron oxide. This powdery substance is not very good at supporting a road bridge! The ironwork needs to be protected from the oxygen in the air to prevent rusting.

Uncontrolled combustion destroys things and endangers lives. You must always take care to avoid things catching fire.

If milk is left in a warm place, bacteria in the milk produce an acid. This reacts with the milk and causes it to go sour. Keeping the milk cold slows this down.

Limescale is a crusty accumulation in pipes, kettles and boilers. It occurs when substances dissolved in the water react. It blocks pipes and causes kettles and boilers to be inefficient. Limescale can be cleaned with vinegar. The chemical reaction results in the formation of a salt, which runs off with water.

FIG 4.16 Chemical reactions are going on everywhere you look

FIG 4.17 Limescale accumulation

Fun fact

Brining is a process in which meat or fish is preserved by soaking in salt water. The high salt content prevents the meat and fish from undergoing decomposition reactions.

Check your understanding

1. Think about the process of a banana ripening. How do you know that a chemical change is taking place?

2. Which of these involves a chemical change?

    a) A wood fire
    b) An electric heater
    c) Boiling water
    d) Boiling an egg
    e) Making a fruit salad
    f) Fruit browning after being cut

Key terms

rusting the process in which iron changes to iron oxide

explosions violent chemical reactions that give off heat and light

limescale a substance formed when chemicals in water react

Solutions

We are learning how to:

- define a mixture
- explain why a solution is a mixture
- name the parts of a solution.

Mixtures »»

A **mixture** is a physical mix of substances. There are various types of mixture. In the following activity, you will make a special type of mixture – a **solution**.

Activity 4.13

Making a solution

Work in a group.

Here is what you need:

- beaker containing 50 cm³ water
- crystals of copper sulfate
- spatula
- stirring rod
- stopwatch.

 SAFETY

Copper sulfate is an irritant and harmful if swallowed.

Here is what you should do:

1. Add a full spatula of crystals to the water and, as you stir them, record the length of time it takes for them to disappear.
2. Repeat for five more full spatulas of crystals.
3. What are you making with the crystals and water?
4. Do you think the crystals and water are chemically reacting?
5. Can you still see the components of the mixture?
6. The 'disappearance time' of the crystals will probably increase for each spatula addition. Suggest why.

FIG 4.18 Copper sulfate crystals added to water results in copper sulfate solution

FIG 4.19 When flour is added to water, it does not result in a solution

Solutions

When crystals are mixed with water and the crystals disappear, the mixture is called a solution. It is not possible to identify the component parts of the mixture, so a solution is defined as **homogeneous** or a uniform mixture of substances. Homogeneous means 'the same throughout'.

When water is used to form a solution, the combination is known as an **aqueous solution** (from the Latin for water, *aqua*).

The disappearance of the crystals was the result of their **dissolving** in the water. The water is referred to as the **solvent** and the crystals as the **solute**. The crystals may colour the liquid (as in Fig 4.18), but the liquid remains clear – you can see through it.

A cloudy liquid – such as when you add flour to water – is a mixture but is not a solution. The flour has not dissolved. You say it is not **soluble**.

Check your understanding

1. Name and define the parts of a solution.
2. State two characteristics of a solution.
3. List some aqueous solutions that are used in the home.

Key terms

mixture a physical mix of substances

solution when one substance is dissolved in another

homogeneous when it is not possible to identify the component parts of the mixture

aqueous solution a solution formed with water

dissolving when a solid substance mixes with a liquid substance and becomes part of the liquid mixture

solvent the liquid in which a substance dissolves

solute the substance that dissolves in a solvent

soluble when a substance is able to dissolve

Dissolving

We are learning how to:

- define concentration
- calculate the concentration of a solution.

Concentration ▶▶▶

Where did the crystals go in Activity 4.13? They could not really 'disappear'.

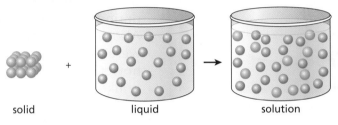

solid + liquid → solution

FIG 4.20 When soluble crystals are added to water they break up into tiny particles that fit into the small spaces between the water molecules

As the amount of crystals increased in Activity 4.13, the time it took for the crystals to dissolve increased. This is because as you increase the amount of solute, the solution becomes more *concentrated*. The amount of available space between the water molecules that can hold the particles of solute decreases.

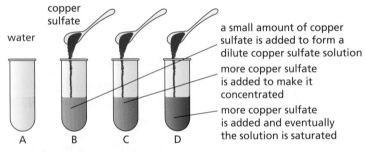

a small amount of copper sulfate is added to form a dilute copper sulfate solution

more copper sulfate is added to make it concentrated

more copper sulfate is added and eventually the solution is saturated

FIG 4.21 A more concentrated solution

Concentration is defined as the mass of solute in a given volume of solvent.

The opposite of a concentrated solution is a **dilute solution**.

Activity 4.14

Calculating concentration

Work in a group. Here is what you need:

- lever arm balance
- measuring cylinder
- crystals (sugar, salt, copper sulfate or Epsom salts)
- possibly a Bunsen burner.
- spatula
- beaker

SAFETY

Wear eye protection goggles for heating. Use correct procedure to light Bunsen burner. Do not touch hot apparatus and materials with bare hands. Care needed with copper sulfate and Epsom salts.

Here is what you should do:

1. Choose a recorder (someone to write down your results) for your group.

2. Measure a volume of water and record.

3. Measure a mass of your crystals and record.

4. Make a solution. If the crystals are taking too long to dissolve, use a gentle yellow Bunsen flame.

5. Find the concentration of your solution:

$$\frac{\text{mass of solute (g)}}{\text{volume of water (cm}^3)}$$

Concentration uses the unit g/cm^3.

Concentration calculations are important in such cases as how much chlorine solution is to be poured into a swimming pool or when a blood thinner should be given to a patient.

Check your understanding

1. Explain the meaning of concentration, using spoonfuls of coffee granules and water as an example.

2. Explain why the more dilute a solution, the greater its ability to dissolve more solute. Draw a picture to help your explanation.

3. Suggest why stirring helps to speed up dissolving.

4. In forming a solution of a required concentration, is it just either the mass of solute or the volume of solvent that matters? Or do you need to know both?

5. Find the concentration of each solution.

   a) 5 g of salt in 90 cm³ of water
   b) 20 g of copper sulfate in 5000 cm³ of water

6. The concentration of a sugar solution is 1.2 g/cm³. How much sugar is in 1500 cm³ of water?

7. How much water was used to make a solution of potassium chloride if the concentration is 0.4 g/cm³ and 5 g of solute was used?

Fun fact

Drivers can be tested for blood alcohol concentration (BAC) using a breathalyser or by analysing a sample of blood, saliva or urine to check whether they are over the legal limit for BAC.

Key terms

concentration mass of solute in a given volume of solvent

dilute solution the opposite of a concentrated solution

Saturated solutions

We are learning how to:

- make a saturated solution
- define saturation
- explain the effect of heating on a saturated solution.

How much solute can dissolve? 》》

Is there a limit to the amount of solute that can be dissolved in a solvent?

Activity 4.15

Making a saturated solution

Work in a group.

Here is what you need:

- beaker containing 50 cm³ water
- crystals of copper sulfate
- spatula
- stirring rod.

 SAFETY

Wear eye protection goggles for heating. Use correct procedure to light Bunsen burner. Do not touch hot apparatus and materials with bare hands. Care needed with copper sulfate.

Here is what you should do:

1. Add a full spatula of crystals to the water and stir.
2. Repeat for five more full spatulas of crystals.
3. Add another spatula of crystals and stir.
4. Repeat this a few more times, until there is undissolved solute in your beaker.
5. Why does this solute remain undissolved?
6. Keep the solution you have made for Activity 4.16.

As more solute is dissolved in a solvent, the solution becomes increasingly concentrated. Eventually it will reach the point when no more solute will be dissolved, however much you stir or however long you wait. The solution is then said to be **saturated**.

Activity 4.16

Heating a saturated solution

Here is what you need:

- your saturated solution and the equipment from Activity 4.15
- tripod
- gauze mat
- Bunsen burner
- heatproof mat
- eye protection.

FIG 4.22 Apparatus for heating a saturated solution

Here is what you should do:

1. Set up your apparatus as shown in Fig 4.22. You should use a very gentle flame. Suggest why.

 SAFETY

Wear eye protection goggles for heating. Use correct procedure to light Bunsen burner. Do not touch hot apparatus and materials with bare hands. Care needed with copper sulfate.

2. Stir the solution and observe. Are there still undissolved crystals present?

3. Add more crystals. Do they dissolve?

4. How many more spatulas of crystals can you dissolve in the solution?

5. Turn off the flame, take the rod from the beaker and carefully place the beaker on the heatproof mat.

6. Can you suggest why it was possible to dissolve more solute in the same amount of solvent after heating?

7. Put the solution to one side to allow it to cool for the next lesson.

Explaining the effect of heat

At room temperature, the solution became saturated when a certain amount of solute had dissolved. Heating the solution made the solvent molecules move about more and move further apart. This created more space to hold solute particles so more solute dissolved. As this extra space filled with more solute particles, the solution became saturated again.

Key term

saturated the inability to dissolve any more solute at a given temperature

Check your understanding

1. Explain why a saturated solution can dissolve no more solute.

Supersaturated solutions

We are learning how to:

- make a supersaturated solution
- grow crystals in a supersaturated solution.

Making crystals 》》

The solution you made last lesson has now cooled. You were able to add extra copper sulfate to the solution when it was hot because hot solvents generally dissolve more solute than cold solvents. If no solid crystallised out on cooling there is more solute dissolved in the solvent than would usually be the case at a lower temperature. The solution is now **supersaturated**.

The excess solute in supersaturated solutions tends to come out of solution and form solid, undissolved crystals.

Activity 4.17

Making crystals

Here is what you need:

- your cooled solution from Activity 4.16, which is now supersaturated
- seed crystal of copper sulfate
- thread
- glass rod or pencil.

Here is what you should do:

1. Tie the seed crystal to one end of the thread.

2. Attach the other end of the thread to the glass rod or pencil and set up as in Fig 4.23.

3. Gently lower the seed crystal into the supersaturated solution and set it aside. Leave for at least 24 hours.

4. Compare what you set up with what you now see. Describe what you have in your beaker.

5. Look at the results of other groups.

6. Can you explain what has happened to the supersaturated solution?

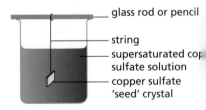

glass rod or pencil

string

supersaturated cop
sulfate solution

copper sulfate
'seed' crystal

FIG 4.23 Apparatus set up with supersaturated solution

FIG 4.24 Examples of crystals formed from supersaturated solutions

What happened to the supersaturated solution?

As the high temperature of a supersaturated solution is reduced, the space between the solvent particles decreases. This makes the solvent no longer able to hold those particles that were dissolved at the higher temperature. As a result, the extra particles **recrystallise** out of the solution.

Making a solution is a physical process as it is possible to reverse the solution to obtain the solute again.

Activity 4.18

Writing a laboratory report

You do not need any equipment for this activity.

Here is what you should do:

1. Discuss with group members the information that should go into a laboratory report of your activities with saturated solutions.

2. Write up the laboratory report.

3. Ensure you make clear conclusions regarding your observations, and explain them scientifically using the key words you have learned.

Check your understanding

1. Explain how you know that dissolving is a physical change.

2. When the copper sulfate crystals were dissolved, was that a physical or chemical change?

3. What effect did heating have on the solution?

4. Why was it possible to retrieve the copper sulfate?

5. What physical property was shown in your experiment?

Fun fact

Supersaturated solutions are used in cooking for making candy, fudges and caramels.

Key term

supersaturated a solution that contains more solute than is required to saturate the solution at that temperature

recrystallise change back into solid form when a supersaturated solution is left for some time

Mixtures

We are learning how to:

- categorise other combinations of substances as mixtures
- identify types of liquid-based mixtures.

Combining substances >>>

Solutions are not the only liquid-based combinations.

Activity 4.19

Combining some substances

You should work in groups of six.

Here is what you need:

- hand lenses
- beakers
- watch-glasses
- measuring cylinder
- trough
- torch
- gloves
- hand mixer or swizzle stick

- soil
- flour
- water
- beakers
- spatulas
- egg
- vinegar
- ketchup

- mustard
- milk powder
- jelly granules
- gummy bears/worms
- mousse
- glue
- dishwashing liquid or soap powder.

Here is what you should do:

1. Mix the following combinations using separate apparatus:

   - jelly granules with water and place in refrigerator

   - soil and water in a beaker

   - three scoops milk powder and 6 cm³ water in a beaker

   - some flour and a few drops of water, enough to thicken on a watch-glass

   - an egg, 5 cm³ vinegar and 2 cm³ water

   - a few drops of dishwashing liquid in half a trough of water and agitate with mixer, swizzle stick or with your hand.

SAFETY
Wear gloves.

2. Allow the combinations to stand undisturbed for a while.

3. Separately place each of the other materials on watch-glasses.

4. After about 40 minutes retrieve the jelly from the refrigerator.

5. Use the torch and hand lens to find the answers to the following:

   a) Are the combinations clear?

   b) Do you think that the liquid dissolved the solid substances?

   c) Explain why you would not call the combinations 'solutions'.

   d) Would you call these combinations 'mixtures'?

All the liquid-based combinations you made were mixtures. All mixtures are physical combinations and have the following properties:

* They do not form a new substance.

* They keep the physical properties of the components that make them.

* It is easy to identify the components that make them.

* Components can usually be separated easily.

FIG 4.25 Examples of liquid-based mixtures

Naming liquid-based mixtures

In all the mixtures you just made, no dissolving occurred.

* A mixture of soil, sand or chalk with water is called a **suspension**.

* A mixture of flour and water is a **paste**.

* Dishwashing liquid and water produce a **foam**.

* Vinegar and egg yolk produce an **emulsion**.

* Jelly crystals and water produce a **gel**.

A suspension is a **heterogeneous mixture**. Pastes, emulsions, gels and foams are homogeneous mixtures. The components cannot be seen easily and no settling occurs. These four are called **colloids**. A colloid is a homogeneous mixture where undissolved solid, liquid or gas are spread through a liquid.

Check your understanding

1. Explain the difference between a suspension and a colloid.

2. Give one similarity between a colloid and a solution.

3. Identify the types of mixtures in the photographs in Fig 4.25.

4. Name as many other liquid-based mixtures as you can that are used in the home. State whether each is a suspension, a paste, a foam or an emulsion.

Key terms

suspension a heterogeneous mixture of undissolved solids that settles on standing

paste a homogeneous opaque mixture of undissolved solid in a liquid

foam a homogeneous mixture of undissolved gas and liquid

emulsion a homogeneous mixture of undissolved liquids

gel a homogeneous translucent mixture of solids in a liquid

heterogeneous mixture a mixture in which all the components can be seen

colloids homogeneous mixtures where no dissolving occurs

Mixtures (2)

We are learning how to:

* name products made from non-liquid-based mixtures.

Solid–solid mixtures »»

Many mixtures of solid and liquid are familiar to us in everyday life.

Soil is an example of a solid–solid mixture and is referred to as a mechanical combination.

Activity 4.20

Looking at alloys and plastics

You need Fig 4.26, which shows examples of some mixtures.

FIG 4.26 Mixtures of solid and solid: **a)** Alloys **b)** Plastics

Here is what you should do:

1. Look at the materials in Fig 4.26.

2. Describe what type of material is an **alloy**. Why is it a mixture?

3. Suggest why there can be so many different types of **plastic**.

Plastics are made from substances called polymers, mixed with plasticisers.

FIG 4.27 Statues are often made from the alloy bronze as it does not rust or corrode

Activity 4.21

Looking at solid–gas mixtures

You need Fig 4.28 showing some more common mixtures.

 a)

 b)

FIG 4.28

Here is what you should do:

1. Decide what the mixtures in Fig 4.28 are.

2. Decide what states of matter were combined to make them.

An aerogel is another mixture of solid with gas.

Gases also mix with each other to form mixtures.

Air is a mixture of gases.

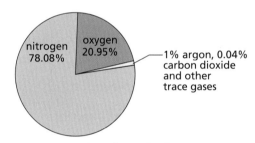

nitrogen 78.08%

oxygen 20.95%

1% argon, 0.04% carbon dioxide and other trace gases

FIG 4.29 Proportion of gases in air

The gases in air are all colourless and odourless. Although air cannot be seen, it supports life, causes changes in weather patterns and provides a medium through which sound can travel. As a mixture, its composition may vary. However, it contains roughly 78 per cent nitrogen and 21 per cent oxygen. The other one per cent is a mixture of various useful gases.

Check your understanding

1. List as many as you can of the following:

   a) solid–solid mixtures

   b) solid–gas mixtures.

2. Air is a mixture of gases. Identify the main gases in air and say in what proportions they are present.

Key terms

alloy a mixture of metals

plastic a group of materials made from products of crude oil

Review of Physical and chemical processes

- Physical properties are characteristics of a substance that can be observed without changing the nature of the substance.

- Qualitative physical properties include colour, odour and state of matter.

- Quantitative physical properties give numerical information about matter and include electrical conductivity, heat conductivity, solubility, melting and boiling point, strength, hardness, elasticity and magnetism.

- Chemical properties are the characteristics shown when a substance combines with another during a chemical change.

- When substances are heated, some undergo a physical change, some a chemical change and others no change.

- A chemical change may be evidenced by smell, colour change, coloured flame, giving out or taking in heat, sound or explosion, or effervescence.

- In a chemical reaction, a new substance is formed with different properties from the starting substances.

- Chemical changes are not usually reversible.

- Chemical changes include the rusting of iron, combustion, decomposition, food digestion, cooking, explosions and fruit ripening.

- Some chemical changes are not desirable and need to be prevented.

- Mixing and changes of state are physical changes, which are reversible.

- A mixture is a physical mix of substances.

- A solution is one type of mixture.

- When crystals are dissolved in water, a homogeneous solution is formed: a uniform mixture of solute (crystals) and solvent (water).

- As more solute dissolves in a solvent, the solution becomes increasingly concentrated.

- The concentration of a solution is calculated as the mass of solute to a given volume of solvent.

- When no more solute can be dissolved, the given volume of solution is said to be saturated, at that particular temperature.

  o More solute can be dissolved in a saturated solution if it is heated.

  o If a heated, saturated solution is left to cool, it becomes supersaturated and can be used to grow crystals of solute.

- Dissolving does not occur in all liquid-based mixtures.

- A suspension is a heterogeneous mixture of a solid in a liquid in which the solid settles on standing.

- Colloids are homogeneous and no settling occurs. These include paste (an opaque mixture of solid and liquid), emulsion (a mixture of two liquids), foam (a mixture of liquid and a gas) and gel (a transparent/translucent mixture of solid and liquid).

- Alloys are a mixture of metals.

- Plastics are a mixture of polymers and plasticisers.

- Smoke and styrofoam are mixtures of solids with gases.

- Mixtures of gases are useful – for example, in breathing apparatus for divers.

Review questions on Physical and chemical processes

1. Explain the difference between qualitative and quantitative properties.

2. State two quantitative properties of a substance and say how each is found.

3. a) Define these terms:
   i) irreversible
   ii) decomposition
   iii) combustion
   iv) effervescence
   v) concentration
   vi) solute
   vii) soluble.

   b) For each, write a scientifically correct sentence that exemplifies the use of the word.

4. a) State three different effects that heat has on matter.
   b) Give an example of each type of effect.

5. Give two examples of evidence that a chemical reaction has occurred.

6. When carrying out experiments, why is it necessary to focus on safety precautions? Use an example of an experiment you have done to help you answer.

7. Explain why making juice is a physical change, not a chemical change.

8. **a)** Why is it that as more and more spoonfuls of crystals are added to a certain volume of solvent, the dissolving time for each spoonful increases?

   b) What will eventually happen to the solution?

9. A saturated solution of salt and water is heated. More salt is added, which dissolves. Explain why, when it returns to room temperature, salt crystals appear.

10. Explain the following terms with examples:

   i) homogeneous

   ii) heterogeneous

   iii) colloid

   iv) suspension.

Unit 5: Separating mixtures

Introduction

Mixtures are physical combinations. This means that the components can be easily identified and are usually easily separated.

The various types of mixture include the following combinations:

- solid–solid
- solid–liquid
- liquid–liquid
- liquid–gas
- gas–gas.

FIG 5.1 Soil samples are examples of solid–solid mixtures

Solid–liquid mixtures include aqueous solutions. As you learned in Unit 4, the concentration of aqueous solutions can be increased such that recrystallisation occurs. This is very useful in the confectionery industry where the concept of recrystallisation is applied in the production of jams, jellies and candy.

Many liquid-based mixtures are not solutions and therefore no dissolving occurs. Combinations such as suspensions, emulsions and pastes are mixtures of this type.

There are many ways to separate physical combinations. The method of separation used depends on the type and size of the components of the mixture. Some methods include evaporation, filtration, chromatography and decanting.

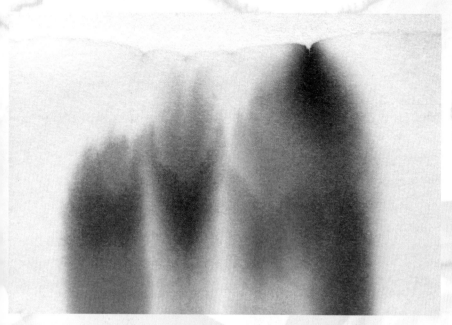

FIG 5.2 Chromatography can be used to separate the coloured pigments in ink

FIG 5.3 Filtration is used to separate the impurities in water to make it fit for human use, in water treatment plants such as this one

Separating mixtures

We are learning how to:

- explain methods of separating mixtures
- choose appropriate methods to separate mixtures
- separate mixtures using hand-picking, sieving or filtration
- name the parts of the mixture obtained after filtration.

Physical separation 〉〉〉

A mixture is a physical combination and can therefore be separated using physical means. How do you do this?

Activity 5.1

Hand-picking, sieving, filtering

Here is what you need:

- mixtures of: stones and seeds, salt and rice, soil and water
- funnel
- filter paper
- glass rod
- sieve
- beaker
- conical flask
- containers
- retort stand with clamp.

FIG 5.4 Different mixtures

Here is what you should do:

1. Decide if you need any apparatus to separate the stones and seeds. Try separating them. Is it easy? Why?

2. Decide if you need apparatus to separate the salt and rice. Try separating them. Which equipment did you use? Why was that a good method?

3. Decide how would you separate the soil and the water. Try separating them. Why did you choose that method? Was your method successful?

The stones are relatively large compared with the seeds, so they can be separated by hand-picking each one out or by using a sieve. Salt grains are much smaller than the rice grains and so a mesh, such as a kitchen sieve, with holes that are too small for the rice to go through, can be used for separation. The method is called **sieving**. Filtration would also work with this mixture.

Filtration

The soil and water can also be separated by sieving, but in this case the 'sieve' is filter paper that has tiny perforations that are much too tiny for the soil particles to go through. This method is called **filtration** or filtering.

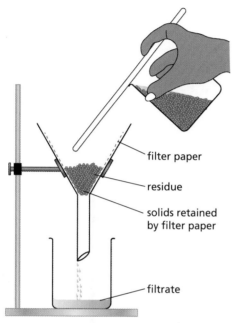

filter paper

residue

solids retained by filter paper

filtrate

FIG 5.5 Separating soil and water by filtration

When the filtration process is complete, the liquid collected is called the **filtrate** and the solid left on the filter paper is called the **residue**. If the perforations of the filter paper were small enough so that not even the tiniest soil particle would go through, the filtrate would be as crystal clear as it was before the mixture was made. However, this is not likely. Filtration is only one part of the process used to purify water for human use.

Check your understanding

1. **a)** A mixture of soil and water is separated by passing through filter paper. Draw a diagram to show how this is done and label the filtrate, the filter and the residue.

   b) Why is the filtrate coloured after the separation?

Key terms

sieving a method of separation where one material is smaller in size than the other

filtration a method of separation using paper with very small perforations (holes)

filtrate material that passes through filter paper

residue material that does not pass through filter paper

Evaporation and distillation

We are learning how to:

- explain methods of separating mixtures
- separate the components of a solid–liquid solution by evaporation and by distillation
- explain how the distillation apparatus works
- outline the advantages and disadvantages of distillation over evaporation.

Evaporation >>>

Activity 5.2

Evaporating a solution

Here is what you need:

- solutions of copper sulfate and/or sodium chloride
- evaporating basin.

Here is what you should do:

1. Pour some of the solution into an evaporating basin until it is half-full.
2. Place the evaporating basin somewhere warm, like a sunny windowsill.
3. Leave the evaporating basin and its contents overnight.
4. Examine the contents of the evaporating basin the following day.
5. Discuss your observations.

FIG 5.6 Apparatus set up for evaporation

In Form 1 you learned that **evaporation** is the process by which a liquid becomes a gas below its boiling point.

When an aqueous solution of crystals dissolved in water is left on a sunny windowsill, the water evaporates and escapes. When evaporation is complete, only the solid is left. Because the solid has been dried very quickly it tends to dry out as a powder, not as crystals. Crystals are only produced with very slow evaporation.

Some liquids evaporate more easily than others. This property is called **volatility**. Very volatile liquids evaporate quickly at room temperature. Perfume is one example.

Distillation

Activity 5.3

Observing distillation (1)

Your teacher will set up the apparatus as shown in Fig 5.7. It is called distillation apparatus and is used to separate a solution.

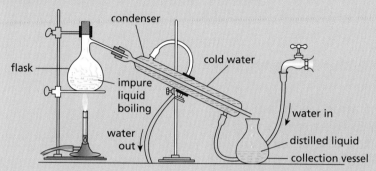

FIG 5.7 Distillation apparatus consists of three main parts: distillation flask, condenser, collection vessel

Here is what you should do:

1. Observe the apparatus set up by your teacher. Observe the demonstration carefully.

Distillation is used in many labs for separating or purifying components of a liquid mixture.

As the impure liquid (solution) is heated, it forms a vapour. The vapour escapes into the condenser where the cooling by the surrounding cold running water causes the vapour to condense back to a liquid. This liquid drips into the collection vessel as the distilled liquid or '**distillate**', while the solid remains as a residue in the distillation flask.

The main advantage of distillation over evaporation is that both the liquid and the solid are retrieved. For use on a large scale, however, it is time- and energy-consuming. A tremendous amount of water is wasted.

Check your understanding

1. Why is it an advantage for a perfume to be volatile?

2. In the distillation apparatus shown in Fig 5.7, suggest why the 'in' water to the condenser is at a lower level than the 'out' water?

3. You have now made crystals by two processes – by cooling a supersaturated solution and by evaporation. Which do you think gives the purer crystals? Why?

Fun fact

Approximately 97 per cent of the water on Earth is salty, and therefore not drinkable. One method of obtaining fresh water is the desalination of seawater, which involves distillation.

Key terms

evaporation the process by which a liquid becomes a gas below its boiling point

volatility the ability of a liquid to evaporate

distillation method of separation that retrieves solid and liquid from a mixture

distillate distilled liquid after distillation process

Distillation of liquid mixtures

We are learning how to:

- explain methods of separating mixtures
- separate two liquids of different boiling points.

Distillation

Activity 5.4

Observing distillation (2)

Your teacher will perform a demonstration using the distillation apparatus shown in Fig 5.8. This time there are two liquids in the flask – alcohol (in this case an alcohol called ethanol) and water. The aim is to separate these. How can this be done?

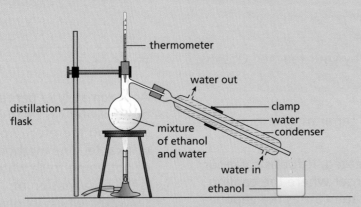

FIG 5.8 Distillation apparatus to separate ethanol from water

Here is what you should do:

1. Observe the demonstration carefully.

2. There is a thermometer in the flask. At what temperature do you observe vaporisation? Ask your teacher what the temperature is on the thermometer.

3. Which one of the liquids is vaporising more quickly? Why?

4. Is there condensation occurring?

5. Does your sense of smell tell you what is condensing?

6. What is happening to the temperature? Can you explain this?

7. Can you tell when all the ethanol is out of the mixture? How?

Ethanol is a volatile liquid that boils at 78 °C. Since the water temperature in the condenser is lower, the ethanol condenses and liquefies. The liquid ethanol drips out into the beaker. The temperature in the flask remains at 78 °C while the ethanol boils. All the heat energy is causing the ethanol to boil. When it has all boiled off, the temperature rises because the water gains energy.

The separation depends on the two liquids having widely different **boiling points**.

FIG 5.9 Rum is made by distilling a fermented molasses mixture. This distillery in Barbados still uses traditional copper distillation apparatus

Check your understanding

1. Complete these sentences by filling in the blank spaces:

   A liquid with a _____ boiling point is a more volatile liquid.

   A liquid with a _____ boiling point is a less volatile liquid.

2. Give two ways in which you can tell that a liquid, when being heated, reaches its boiling point.

3. A mixture of water and another type of alcohol, whose boiling point is 97 °C, needs to be separated. Can distillation be used? Explain your answer.

Key term
....

boiling point the temperature at which a liquid boils and the liquid turns to vapour

Fractional distillation

We are learning how to:

- explain methods of separating mixtures
- explain how fractional distillation occurs
- describe how crude oil is separated.

Fractional distillation ▶▶▶

Look at the apparatus in Fig 5.10, which may be set up and demonstrated by your teacher. It is called a **fractional distillation** apparatus and is used to separate a mixture of liquid components that boil at different temperatures. This method makes use of a fractionating column, which is much more efficient at separating the liquids. It allows liquids with close boiling points to be separated.

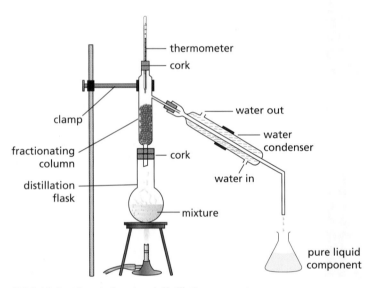

thermometer
cork
clamp
water out
fractionating column
water condenser
cork
distillation flask
water in
mixture
pure liquid component

FIG 5.10 Small-scale fractional distillation apparatus

As the vapours from the distillation flask go up along a vertical **fractionating column**, the temperature in the column decreases. The liquid with the higher boiling point condenses and trickles back to the flask, while the one with a lower boiling point remains as vapour and enters the condenser. It condenses on passing through the condenser and the liquid passes out into a collection vessel.

Fractional distillation in industry

Crude oil is a mixture. It is separated into many useful components using fractional distillation, in the following steps:

1. The crude oil is heated to 400 °C and most of it vaporises.

2. The vapour rises through a fractionating column.

3. As the vapour rises it cools. The higher up the fractionating column it goes, the cooler it gets.

4. When the vapour of a particular component reaches the height where the temperature is just below its boiling point, the vapour condenses to a liquid.

5. A tray at that height collects the liquid, which then flows out into a storage tank.

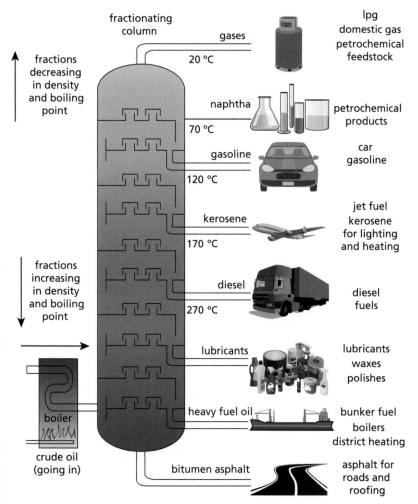

FIG 5.11 Fractional distillation of crude oil showing temperature at which each component boils off

Fun fact

Crude oil was first pumped from the ground 2500 years ago in China.

Key terms

fractional distillation method of separation used to separate a mixture of liquid components that boil at different temperatures

fractionating column part of fractional distillation apparatus where liquid with the higher boiling point condenses and trickles back to the flask

crude oil mixture of chemicals that are the basis of petrochemical industry

Check your understanding

1. Explain why the products that come out at the top of the fractionating column are gases, not liquids.

2. Draw a flowchart to show the steps by which diesel fuel and gasoline are separated in a fractionating column.

Chromatography

We are learning how to:

- explain methods of separating mixtures
- set up a chromatography experiment
- explain how chromatography works.

Chromatography ⟩⟩⟩

Many coloured inks are not pure colours but mixtures. Do you know how many colours make up the ink in a black or brown marker pen? It is easy to separate the ink to reveal its component colours using the method of **chromatography**.

Activity 5.5

Separating inks

Here is what you need:

- sheets of chromatography or filter paper
- beakers
- covers
- ethanol
- markers of various colours
- paperclips, pencils (or lollipop sticks or twigs)
- scissors.

Here is what you should do:

1. Cut the filter paper into long rectangular strips so that each group member gets one strip.

2. Place a dot of marker ink (diameter about 2 mm) at a point about 1 cm from the end of your strip.

3. Place the paperclip at the other end of the filter paper.

4. Attach the paperclip to the pencil.

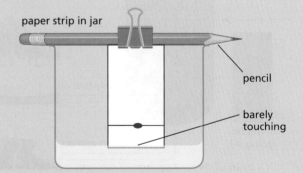

FIG 5.12 Apparatus set up for chromatography

5. Pour a little ethanol into the beaker and lower your strip in so that the strip is a little below the level of the ethanol as shown in Fig 5.12.

6. Cover the beaker (to reduce evaporation of the volatile ethanol) and observe.

7. Discuss what you think will happen to the dot of ink after the paper has been left for a while in the ethanol. (Hint: ink is soluble in ethanol.)

8. You can begin to write up a laboratory report while you wait. Leave space in your observation section to paste your chromatography result when has dried.

How chromatography works

Chromatography is a process in which a mixture, carried through a medium by a liquid (or gas), is separated into its components, because they move through the medium at different rates.

When the pigments in ink are separated using chromatography, ethanol is used as a **solvent**. The pigments have different **solubilities** – they dissolve in the ethanol to different extents. This means that they are carried up the paper at different rates, and some travel further than others.

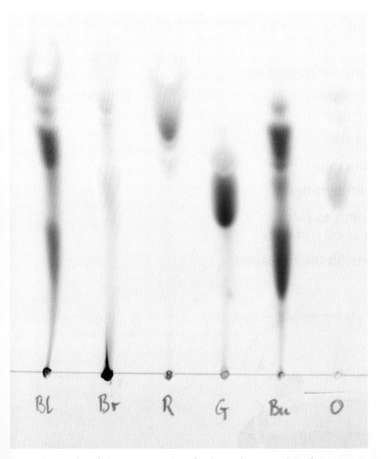

FIG 5.13 Results of chromatography of coloured pens and markers

Check your understanding

1. In your chromatography activity:

   a) What is the 'medium' through which the ink is carried?

   b) What is it carried by?

2. How do you think the coloured patterns in Fig 5.13 were produced?

Key terms

chromatography a process in which a mixture, carried through a medium by a liquid (or gas), is separated into its components, because they move through the medium at different rates

solvent substance in which something dissolves

solubility how much something dissolves in a solvent

Separating liquids

We are learning how to:

- explain methods of separating mixtures
- describe methods of separation that rely on the density of the components
- explain how a separating funnel is used.

Separation and liquid density

There are several separation processes that work because the component substances have different densities. These methods are used widely in industry, food manufacture and medicine.

You should recall from Form 1 that **density** is the mass per unit volume of a substance.

Decanting

The process of **decanting** is used to separate:

- a mixture of a liquid and an insoluble solid
- two **immiscible liquids** with different densities.

Immiscible liquids are those that cannot mix to form a homogeneous (uniform) mixture – such as oil and water.

In both cases the components form layers, so the top layer can be carefully poured off.

FIG 5.14 Decanting is important in the wine industry to prevent the wine mixing with the bitter solid sediment

Separating funnel

A **separating funnel** is another piece of apparatus used to separate a mixture of immiscible liquids, such as an oil and water or aqueous solution. The oil is less dense and floats on the aqueous solution. The stopcock (Fig 5.15) allows the aqueous solution to be drained off.

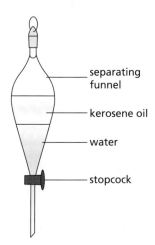

separating funnel

kerosene oil

water

stopcock

FIG 5.15 Liquids for separation in a separating funnel

Using a separating funnel

This is a demonstration experiment involving three students.

One student will be given a beaker with cooking oil, another a beaker with water and a third a large empty beaker.

Here is what you should do:

1. Observe as they pour the oil and the water into the large beaker and stir.

2. Do they mix well? Explain why you think that.

3. How would you separate the oil and water?

4. Observe as the mixture is poured into the apparatus.

5. What do you notice as it stands undisturbed? Why?

6. Observe a student placing a beaker under the pipe and slowly opening the stopcock.

7. What drains into the beaker? Why?

8. Is it possible to drain out all the water? Why?

Check your understanding

1. Explain how to use a separating funnel to separate two liquids.

Fun fact

A gravy separator is a kitchen utensil that is used to separate meat juices from fat. The hot meat juices and any hot meat stock containing fat are poured into the separator and the fat rises to the top, while the layers of meat juices remain on the bottom.

Key terms

density mass per unit volume of a substance

decanting process used to separate a mixture of a liquid and an insoluble solid or two immiscible liquids of different densities

immiscible liquids liquids that cannot mix to form a homogeneous (uniform) mixture, such as oil and water

separating funnel piece of apparatus used to separate a mixture of immiscible liquids

Other methods of separating mixtures

We are learning how to:

- explain methods of separating mixtures
- describe methods of separation that rely on the density of the components.

Centrifugation ⟩⟩

Centrifugation is a process that involves the use of high speed rotation in a **centrifuge** to separate two immiscible liquids, or a sediment and a liquid. The denser component migrates further away from the centre (axis) of the centrifuge, while the less dense component migrates less far from the centre.

Centrifugation has many applications in many different fields. Some are outlined below.

Medicine

- DNA preparation
- Purifying the contents of bronchus fluids
- Separating blood serum and fats

Industry

- Separation of oils and waxes at oil refineries

Food

- Separating the cream from skimmed milk
- Butter oil purification
- Removing solid impurities from milk
- Isolating sugar crystals from molasses

In the home

- In bagless vacuum cleaners
- Rinsing and drying clothes in the washing machine

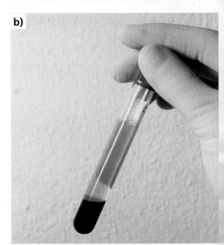

FIG 5.16 **a)** A centrifuge can be used to separate the components of blood **b)** Results of separating components of blood

In the manufacture of cane sugar, centrifugation is used to separate the sediments from the juice.

FIG 5.18 Modern centrifuges in a sugar mill

Sedimentation

Gravity causes **insoluble** solids that are suspended in water to settle out. The solids are denser than the water and so sink to the bottom as **sediment**. This process of **sedimentation** is used in reservoirs as the initial cleaning process of water collected from rivers.

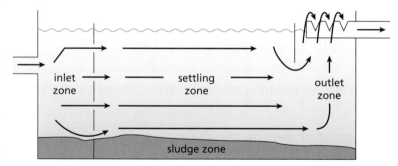

FIG 5.17 A sedimentation chamber

Check your understanding

1. Which method of separation would be suitable for the following mixtures? There may be more than one answer for each.

   a) A mixture of cooking oil and vinegar
   b) A mixture of gravel and water
   c) The components of guava juice
   d) Whole milk (into cream and skimmed milk)
   e) Honey and honeycomb

Key terms

centrifugation a process that involves the use of high speed rotation in a centrifuge to separate two immiscible liquids, or a sediment and a liquid

centrifuge apparatus used in centrifugation

insoluble solids that do not dissolve

sediment insoluble solids that settle at the bottom of liquids

sedimentation process by which insoluble solids sink to the bottom of a liquid

Review of Separating mixtures

- A mixture is a physical combination and can therefore be separated using physical means.

- There are various methods of separating a mixture, each based on the physical properties of the components – for example: particle size, volatility and boiling point, solubility, density.

- The methods of separation that depend on particle size are: filtration, sieving and hand-picking.

- In filtration, a mixture of a solid and a liquid are passed through a filter. The liquid collected is the filtrate and the solid left on the filter is called the residue.

- The methods of separation that depend on volatility and boiling point are: evaporation, distillation and fractional distillation.

- The more volatile a liquid, the lower its boiling point. A very volatile liquid evaporates at room temperature.

- In distillation apparatus, a liquid is boiled off and then its vapour is condensed.

- Simple distillation can be used to separate the solid and liquid components of a solution, or two liquids with very different boiling points.

- Fractional distillation is needed to separate liquids of similar boiling points.

- In a fractionating column, the more volatile liquids are collected further up the column.

- The method of separation that depends on the solubility of the components is chromatography.

- Different inks dissolve at different rates in ethanol, so they travel different distances up the chromatography paper.

- The methods of separation that depend on density are: decanting, use of a separating funnel, centrifugation and sedimentation.

Review questions on Separating mixtures

1. Match the letter assigned to each description with the number of the method it describes.

	Method		Description
1	centrifugation	a	method by which particle size is separated
2	fractional distillation	b	only the solid is left
3	sieving	c	method used for separation of dyes
4	decanting	d	rotational speed is required
5	evaporation	e	used for separating the parts of a solution
6	sedimentation	f	wine undergoes this separation
7	filtration	g	separation of a mixture of liquids of similar but different boiling points
8	distillation	h	occurs at water treatment plants
9	chromatography	i	natural separation of liquid and insoluble solid that sinks to the bottom

TABLE 5.1

2. You have a mixture of pebbles, sand, salt and iron filings, all in water. Explain how you would separate the mixture into its five different components.

3. a) Describe how fractional distillation works.

   b) Explain how products are obtained from crude oil.

4. Name:

   a) one advantage of distillation compared with evaporation

   b) one disadvantage of distillation compared with evaporation.

5. Explain how separation occurs in the process of chromatography.

6. a) When is a separating funnel used?

   b) Explain how this apparatus works.

7. Draw and label a diagram to show how sedimentation occurs.

8. Describe how centrifugation works.

Investigating pigments in leaves

Plants are green because they contain the pigment chlorophyll. This pigment is essential for the process of photosynthesis. Not all plants have green leaves. Does this mean that they do not contain chlorophyll?

The answer is no, because if the leaves of a plant did not contain chlorophyll they would not be able to make food and therefore would not exist. They do contain chlorophyll but it is masked by other pigments. For example, the presence of pigments called anthocyanins can result in red, blue or purple colouration of leaves.

1. You are going to work in a group of three or four to investigate the pigments present in non-green leaves. The tasks are:

   - to identify local examples of plants that do not have green, or totally green, leaves
   - to devise a method of extracting the colouring matter from leaves
   - to separate the different pigments found in the leaves of a particular plant
   - to separate and then count the number of pigments present.

   a) Look at the leaves of plants found growing locally on open ground, perhaps in gardens or maybe as pot plants.

   What are the names of these plants? Can you find the Latin name as well as the local name?

   Make arrangements to obtain a sample of leaves. If the plants are on open ground, you may just take the leaves. If they are in a garden or on a potted plant, you should ask the permission of the owner. Explain that this won't cause the plants any harm.

   b) How are you going to extract the coloured pigments from the leaf cells? You need to consider:

   - How to crush the plant material. Maybe you could use a mortar and pestle?

FIG 5.SIP.1 Not all plant leaves are green

- How to extract the pigments from the crushed plant material. Are the pigments soluble in a small amount of water or would another solvent be better? What other solvents are available?

- How to separate the extract from the remaining plant material.

c) You are going to use chromatography to separate the pigments in your extract. Look back at Topic 5.6 and make sure that you understand this method of separation. You need to decide such things as:

- the apparatus you will need
- the solvent to use.

FIG 5.SIP.2 A mortar and pestle can be used to crush plant material

d) Are there any ways you might improve the separation of the pigments? For example, does the separation improve if you use longer strips of chromatography paper?

When you carry out the chromatography you might find that the solvent you are using works with the leaves of some plants and not others. You might decide to experiment with different solvents in order to improve the separation of pigments.

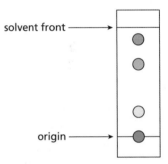

FIG 5.SIP.3 Separating pigments

e) How are you going to make comparisons between the leaves of different plants?
You might:

- count the number of spots of different pigments for each plant
- take photographs of your chromatograms and display them in order of number of pigments.

f) Can you find out the names of some of the different coloured pigments you discover in your leaves? You might try searching on the internet by typing in the name of the plant followed by 'leaf pigments' or 'colour of leaves'.

g) Give a slideshow presentation to the class on what you have found out about the different pigments found in plant leaves. Your presentation should:

- include a table of how many pigments were detected in the leaves of each plant
- be illustrated with some pictures of the chromatograms you obtained
- identify which coloured pigment was the most common and which was the least common in the leaves you investigated
- give the names of any pigments you have been able to identify.

Unit 6: Motion

Introduction »»

Motion is about how objects move or are moved in relation to other objects.

Speed

Races start from one point and end at another. All the runners start running at the same time.

FIG 6.1 The winning team has run at a greater speed and, as a result, they have covered the distance in a shorter time

In this unit you are going to look at the relationship between distance, speed and time.

Velocity and acceleration

Is velocity just another word for speed or does it mean something different in science?

FIG 6.2 Some sports cars can accelerate from 0 to 100 km/h in only a few seconds

What is acceleration and how is it different from velocity?

Newton's laws of motion

Legend has it that Sir Isaac Newton was inspired to propose his laws of motion when watching an apple falling from a tree.

We will look at Newton's three laws of motion, and explain how they help us to understand the way in which objects move.

Moments

When a force acts about a point this creates a moment. A moment is the turning effect of a force.

A lever is a simple machine that uses moments.

Why is it that you cannot crack a nut by squeezing it with your fingers but you can by squeezing a nutcracker?

Stability

How is it that some objects are stable while others tip over very easily? Is it possible to predict when an object is likely to tip over?

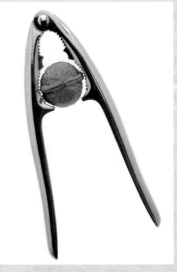

FIG 6.3 A nutcracker is a lever, a simple machine that uses moments

FIG 6.4 As of August 2015, Kelly Ann Baptiste's best time for the 100 m was 10.83 s. This means that she could run at an average speed of 33.24 km/h

Challenge

Athletes are running faster than ever before. Fifty years ago, the world record for running 100 m was 10.06 seconds. Today the record is 9.58 seconds. What will the record be fifty years from now?

Speed

We are learning how to:

- investigate motion of a body
- measure time and distance.

High speed or low speed? >>>

When you travel from one place to another you may move quickly or you may move slowly.

FIG 6.5 Runners in a race move very quickly (they move at a high speed)

FIG 6.6 People out for a stroll move slowly (they move at a low speed)

Speed is a measure of how quickly somebody or something travels the distance between two points. One way to measure speed is to count the number of metres that a person travels each second. This is written as metres per second, **m/s**, or m s^{-1}.

A runner might travel 10 metres each second, which is a speed of 10 m/s, while somebody out for a stroll might only travel one metre each second, which is a speed of 1 m/s.

Activity 6.1

Moving slowly and moving quickly

Here is what you need:

- measuring tape
- two pegs
- stopwatch.

Here is what you should do:

1. Place a peg in the ground.
2. Measure a distance of 100 m from the peg using a measuring tape.

3. Place a second peg in the ground.

4. Time how long it takes you to walk slowly from one peg to the other.

5. Next, time how long it takes you to run quickly from one peg to the other.

6. How much longer did you take to walk the distance than you took to run the same distance?

Cars usually move much more quickly than people. You could measure the number of metres a car travels each second but it is usually more convenient to measure the number of kilometres it travels each hour. This is written as kilometres per hour, **km/h** or km h^{-1}.

Cars are fitted with instruments called speedometers, which indicate their speed.

FIG 6.7 Cars are fitted with instruments called speedometers, which indicate their speed

Check your understanding

1. Look at the speedometer in Fig 6.7.

   a) At what speed is this car travelling?

   b) How far would it go if it travelled at this speed for one hour?

   c) Is the car moving slowing or quickly?

2. Make a list of things that move quickly and a list of things that move slowly. Give your answer in the form of a table.

Things that move quickly	Things that move slowly

TABLE 6.1

Key terms

speed a measure of how quickly somebody or something travels the distance between two points

m/s (or m s^{-1}) number of metres travelled in a second, a unit of speed

km/h (or km h^{-1}) number of kilometres travelled in an hour, a unit of speed

Relationship between speed, distance and time

We are learning how to:

- investigate motion of a body
- calculate speed.

Calculating speed »

You can express the relationship between speed, distance and time in the form of a simple mathematical equation.

$$\text{speed (m/s)} = \frac{\text{distance (m)}}{\text{time (s)}}$$

The unit of speed depends on the units in which distance and time are given. If distance was expressed in kilometres and time in hours, then the unit of speed would be kilometres per hour or km/h.

When a person moves from one place to another their speed seldom remains the same. They might speed up for some parts of their journey and slow down for others.

FIG 6.8 In a 100 m race, the runner starts running slowly, increases their speed to a maximum at between 50 to 60 metres into the race, and then starts to slow down as they get tired

FIG 6.9 A journey by car is not at a constant speed. For some parts of the journey the driver can travel quickly but for others he or she must slow down or stop

When you divide the distance travelled by the time taken, you are finding their **average speed** over the journey.

Worked example 6.1

A motorist travels between two towns that are 200 km apart. The journey takes 2.5 hours. What is the average speed over the journey?

Solution

You do not know whether the motorist is travelling at a constant speed for the whole of the journey or if he or she goes faster at some times and slower at others. But since you know both the total distance and the total time taken you can find the average speed.

$$\text{average speed} = \frac{200 \text{ km}}{2.5 \text{ h}} = 80 \text{ km/h}$$

Sometimes it may be necessary to rearrange the equation. For example, you may wish to find the distance travelled by an object when you know its speed and the time it travels.

Multiplying both sides of the equation by time gives:

$$\text{speed} \times \text{time} = \frac{\text{distance}}{\cancel{\text{time}}} \times \cancel{\text{time}}$$

$$\text{distance} = \text{speed} \times \text{time}$$

Worked example 6.2

A ball travels at a constant speed of 3 m/s for 5 s. How far does the ball travel?

Solution

In this question you are given the speed and the time so you need the form of the equation that lets you work out the distance.

$$\text{distance} = 3 \text{ m/s} \times 5 \text{ s} = 15 \text{ m}$$

Check your understanding

1. **a)** An aircraft travels 7150 km from London to Port of Spain in a time of 11 hours. What was the average speed of the aircraft for the journey?

    b) Make time the subject of the equation relating speed, distance and time.

    c) Calculate the time for the same journey if the speed of the aircraft was increased to 700 km/h.

Fun fact

FIG 6.10 Usain Bolt

As of August 2015, Usain Bolt held the world record for running 100 m in a time of 9.58 s. His average speed during the race was therefore $\frac{100}{9.58} = 10.44$ m/s.

Key term

average speed speed calculated from dividing distance travelled by time taken

Distance–time graphs

We are learning how to:

- investigate motion of a body
- draw and interpret distance–time graphs.

Distance–time graphs »»

You can represent the movement of an object as a graph by plotting the distance it has travelled at different times on its journey.

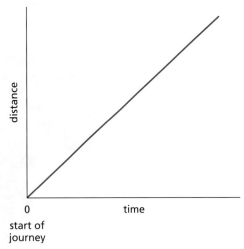

FIG 6.11 Distance–time graph of object moving at constant speed

The shape of a **distance–time graph** depends on how the object moves. If an object moves at a constant speed, the distance–time graph will be a straight line.

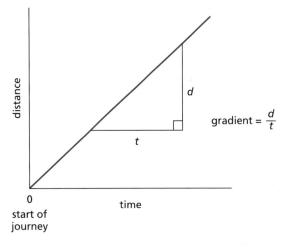

FIG 6.12 Gradient of a distance–time graph

The speed of an object moving at constant speed is given by the slope or gradient of the distance–time graph.

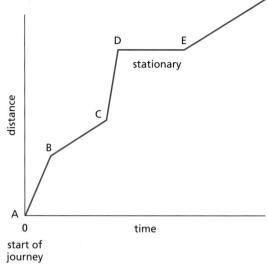

FIG 6.13 The speed is not the same between points A and B as it is between points B and C, points C and D and after point E

If an object changes speed as it moves, the graph will no longer be a straight line. If part of the graph is horizontal (as it is between points D and E), this means that the object is stationary for that period of time and the distance from the start of the journey remains unchanged.

Check your understanding

1. On a distance–time graph:

a) what information is given by the gradient of the graph?

b) how can you tell that an object is stationary?

Fun fact

If a distance–time graph is a curve, the speed at any point can be found by drawing a straight line or tangent to the curve at that point, and calculating its slope.

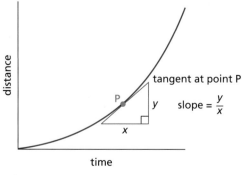

FIG 6.14

Key term

distance–time graph
graph that shows how the distance travelled varies with time

Displacement and velocity

We are learning how to:

- investigate motion of a body
- account for displacement and velocity both in terms of magnitude and direction.

Magnitude and direction

Distance and speed are both examples of scalar quantities. They have size or magnitude but they do not have a particular direction. For example, you might say that a ball travels at 0.5 m/s. You have not specified in which direction, therefore 0.5 m/s represents its speed and in one second it will travel a distance of 0.5 m.

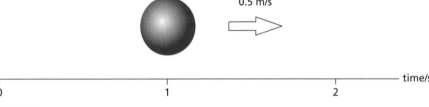

FIG 6.15

The ball in Fig 6.15 is travelling from left to right. The motion of the ball now has both magnitude and direction so you can say that the ball travels at a velocity of 0.5 m/s from left to right, and in one second it will be displaced to the right by a distance of 0.5 m.

Displacement and **velocity** are examples of vector quantities. They have both magnitude and direction.

- Displacement is the distance travelled in a particular direction.

- Velocity is the speed in a particular direction.

Activity 6.2

Measuring your velocity

You should work with a partner for this activity.

Here is what you need:

- measuring tape
- two pegs
- stopwatch.

Here is what you should do:

1. Place a peg in the ground.

2. Measure a distance of 100 m from the peg using a measuring tape in a direction given by your teacher.

3. Place a second peg in the ground.

4. Time how long it takes your partner to walk from the first peg to the second peg in the given direction.

5. Calculate your partner's velocity when they walked.

6. Next, time how long it takes your partner to run from the first peg to the second peg in the given direction.

7. Calculate your partner's velocity when they ran.

8. When was your partner's velocity greater?

FIG 6.17 Rockets need to have a high velocity

When a rocket is launched it travels upwards. You talk about its velocity rather than its speed because it travels in a particular direction. In order to overcome the pull of the Earth's gravity, a rocket must achieve a velocity of 11.2 km/s. This is called the escape velocity. If it does not achieve this velocity it will fall back down to the ground when it runs out of fuel.

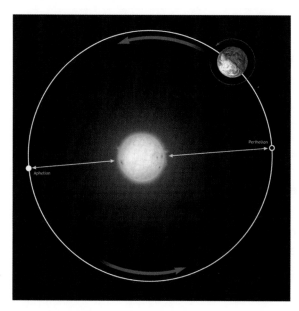

FIG 6.16 The Earth is in orbit around the Sun

The Earth is in orbit around the Sun at a constant speed of 30 km/s. You cannot say that the Earth has a constant velocity of 30 km/s because its direction is continually changing. To have a constant velocity, an object would need to travel both at the same speed and in the same direction.

Check your understanding

1. **a)** Explain the difference between speed and velocity.

   b) The Moon orbits the Earth at a constant speed of about 1 km/s. Why is it incorrect to say that the Moon orbits the Earth at a constant velocity?

Key terms

displacement the distance travelled in a particular direction

velocity the speed in a particular direction

Acceleration

We are learning how to:

- investigate motion of a body
- explain acceleration as a change in velocity.

Changing velocity

An object accelerates when the forces acting on it are not balanced. This may result in the velocity of the object increasing or decreasing. A decrease in velocity is called deceleration.

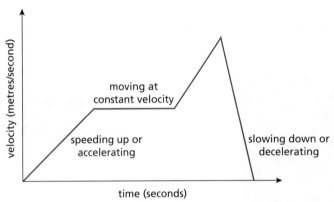

FIG 6.18 A velocity–time graph shows how the velocity of an object changes over time

The shape of the graph indicates how the velocity of the object is changing.

- When the graph is sloping upwards the velocity of the object is increasing; the object is accelerating.

- When the graph is horizontal the object is moving with a constant velocity.

- When the graph is sloping downwards the velocity of the object is decreasing; the object is decelerating.

Acceleration is the rate of change of velocity with respect to time. You can express the relationship between acceleration, velocity and time in the form of a simple mathematical equation.

$$\text{acceleration (m/s}^2) = \frac{\text{change in velocity (m/s)}}{\text{time (s)}}$$

When velocity is expressed in metres per second, and time in seconds, the unit of acceleration is the metre per second per second **m/s²** (or m s⁻²).

The acceleration of a moving object over a period of time is given by the gradient of the velocity–time graph over that period.

Key terms

acceleration rate of change of velocity with respect to time

m/s² (or m s⁻²) units of acceleration

Worked example 6.3

Fig 6.19 shows the velocity of an object over a period of 10 s.

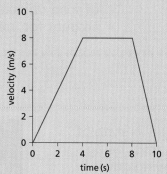

FIG 6.19

What is the acceleration of the object between these times?

  a) 0–4 s   **b)** 4–8 s   **c)** 8–10 s

Solution

The equation you use is:

$$\text{acceleration} = \frac{\text{change in velocity}}{\text{time}}$$

a) acceleration = $\dfrac{8 - 0}{4}$ = 2 m/s²

b) acceleration = $\dfrac{8 - 8}{4}$ = 0 m/s² (so the object is at constant velocity)

c) acceleration = $\dfrac{0 - 8}{2}$ = – 4 m/s² (negative acceleration is deceleration)

Worked example 6.4

How long will it take a car to slow from 30 m/s to 12 m/s if it decelerates at a rate of 1.5 m/s²?

Solution

$$\text{time} = \frac{\text{change in velocity}}{\text{acceleration}} = \frac{30 - 12}{1.5} = \frac{18}{1.5} = 12 \text{ s}$$

Check your understanding

  1. In order for the space shuttle *Discovery* to reach the minimum altitude required to orbit the Earth, it had to accelerate from 0 to a velocity of 8000 m/s in 8.5 minutes.

    a) How many seconds are there in 8.5 minutes?

    b) Calculate the acceleration over this period in m/s², assuming it is constant.

Fun fact

FIG 6.20

A top fuel dragster can accelerate from 0 to 576 m/s in 0.8 seconds. That is an acceleration of 720 m/s².

Inertia and momentum

We are learning how to:

- apply Newton's laws to explain motion of solid objects
- account for inertia.

Inertia ⟫⟫

Inertia is the resistance of an object to change its state of motion. The object might be stationary and resist being moved, or it might be moving and resist slowing down or stopping.

The inertia of an object depends on its **mass**. A heavy object has a large inertia while a light object has a small inertia.

Momentum

Momentum is the product of an object's mass and its velocity. The unit of momentum is therefore the kilogram metre per second, kg m/s.

momentum (kg m/s) = mass (kg) × velocity (m/s)

Notice that momentum is a vector quantity because it has both size and direction. The direction of an object's momentum is the same as its velocity.

The momentum of an object depends on both its mass and its velocity. The larger the mass, the greater the momentum. The larger the velocity, the greater the momentum.

FIG 6.21 All objects have inertia

FIG 6.22 Although a bullet only has a small mass, it has a large momentum because it moves through the air at a very high velocity

FIG 6.23 A super tanker moves much more slowly than a bullet, but it has a huge mass so it also has a large momentum

Worked example 6.5

A smooth bore cannon fires balls of mass 30 kg. The velocity of a ball when leaving the cannon is 480 m/s.

FIG 6.24

What is the momentum of a cannon ball as it leaves the cannon?

Solution

momentum = mass × velocity = 30 × 480 = 14 400 kg m/s

Check your understanding

1. A family car of mass 1400 kg travels down a road at a velocity of 48 km/h.

   a) What is 48 km/h expressed in m/s?

   b) What is the momentum of the car?

2. A bullet of mass 10 g travels at a speed of 360 m/s. What is the momentum of the bullet in kg m/s?

Fun fact

It takes a fully loaded super tanker about 20 minutes to stop when travelling at normal velocity. Because of their large momentum, super tankers turn off their engines about 25 km away from their dock.

Key terms

inertia resistance of an object to change its state of motion

mass the amount of substance an object has

momentum the product of an object's mass and its velocity

Newton's first law of motion

We are learning how to:

- apply Newton's laws to explain motion of solid objects
- apply Newton's first law of motion.

Newton's first law ▶▶▶

A ball returning to the ground can be explained by thinking about the forces acting on it. Air resistance opposes the ball's movement through the air and gravity pulls the ball towards the ground.

In the 17th century, a scientist called Sir Isaac Newton studied the motion of objects and proposed his three laws of motion. **Newton's first law of motion** states that:

A body will remain in a state of rest or uniform motion in a straight line unless it is acted on by an external force.

Newton's first law tells us that:

- an object that is not moving will remain stationary unless a force acts on it

- an object that is moving will continue to move in a straight line at the same speed unless a force acts on it.

The tendency of an object to remain stationary, or to keep moving at a constant speed in a straight line, is called its inertia. In order to overcome inertia a force must be applied.

People travelling in a car have inertia. According to Newton's first law, if the car stops suddenly the driver and passengers will tend to keep on moving at the same speed in the same direction.

FIG 6.25 If you throw a ball into the air it will rapidly fall back to the ground. You provide the force that sends the ball up but why does it come back down?

FIG 6.26 Crash dummy thrown through the windscreen of a car

If the people in the car are not wearing seatbelts, they may end up going through the windscreen and being seriously injured. A seatbelt exerts a force that stops a person from being thrown forward.

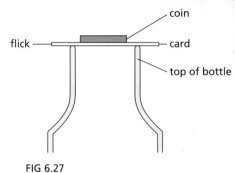

FIG 6.27

Activity 6.3

Newton's first law

Here is what you need:

- beaker
- bottle
- teaspoon
- piece of card
- coin small enough to fit into the bottle.

Here is what you should do.

Part 1

1. Put some water into the beaker.
2. Stir the water with a spoon.
3. Stop stirring and remove the spoon quickly.
4. Describe what happens to the water.
5. Explain your observation in terms of Newton's first law.

Part 2

1. Put the piece of card on top of the bottle.
2. Put the coin on top of the card.
3. Flick the card horizontally with your finger.
4. Describe what happens to the card and to the coin.
5. Explain your observation using Newton's first law.

Check your understanding

Explain the following using Newton's first law of motion.

1. You are riding a bicycle along the road.
   a) You stop pedalling but the bicycle carries on moving for a while.
   b) You brake suddenly. The bicycle stops but you tip over the handlebars.
2. It takes a bigger force to increase the speed of a heavy truck than a small car.
3. The Earth orbits around the Sun in a curved orbit and does not fly off in a straight line into space.

Fun fact

In 1971 the American astronaut Alan Shepard landed on the Moon and used a golf club to hit golf balls. He jokingly said that they went for 'miles and miles and miles'.

FIG 6.28 A golf ball travels much further on the Moon than on the Earth because the Moon has no atmosphere, so no air resistance, and the gravity on the Moon is only about one sixth that on Earth

Key term

Newton's first law of motion a body will remain in a state of rest or uniform motion in a straight line unless it is acted on by an external force

Newton's second law of motion

We are learning how to:

- apply Newton's laws to explain motion of solid objects
- apply Newton's second law of motion.

Newton's second law

Activity 6.4

Effects of a force on motion

Here is what you need:

- mug or other container with a handle
- force meter
- sand
- coloured tape.

Here is what you should do.

1. Mark two points about 10 cm in from the ends of a long table.

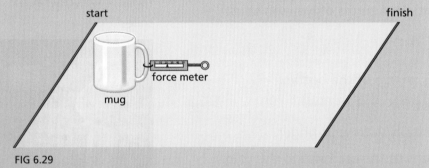

FIG 6.29

2. Place the empty mug on the start line and pull it slowly across the table. Make a note of the reading on the force meter.

3. Replace the empty mug on the start line and pull it quickly across the table. Make a note of the reading on the force meter.

4. Was the force needed to pull the mug quickly less than, equal to or greater than the force needed to pull the mug slowly?

5. Repeat steps 2 and 3, firstly with the mug half full and then with the mug completely full of sand.

6. Was the force needed to pull a half full and a full mug less than, equal to or greater than the force needed to pull an empty mug?

FIG 6.30 When you hit a tennis ball, you are applying a force that will change its motion and the harder you hit the ball the faster it will accelerate away from you

FIG 6.31 If the same force is applied to a shot (mass 4 kg) and to a football (mass about 0.4 kg), the acceleration of the football will be much greater

Newton's second law of motion states that:

When a force acts on an object, it will accelerate in the direction of the force. The amount of acceleration is directly proportional to the force applied and inversely proportional to the mass of the object.

This can be expressed as an equation:

force (N) = mass (kg) × acceleration (m/s^2)

Newton's second law tells us that:

- the bigger the force applied to an object, the more it will accelerate
- for a given force, the bigger the mass of the object, the less it will accelerate.

Check your understanding

1. A ping pong ball has a mass of 2.7 g. A pebble of the same volume has a mass of 54.0 g. When a force is applied to the ping pong ball it accelerates by 1.0 m/s^2.

   a) Explain why, if the same force was applied to the pebble, it would not accelerate by the same amount.

   b) What would be the acceleration of the pebble?

2. A football with a mass of 0.45 kg is kicked with a force of 58 N. How fast will it accelerate?

Key term

Newton's second law of motion when a force acts on an object, it will accelerate in the direction of the force. The amount of acceleration is directly proportional to the force applied and inversely proportional to the mass of the object

Newton's third law of motion

We are learning how to:

- apply Newton's laws to explain motion of solid objects
- apply Newton's third law of motion.

Newton's third law ≫

Have you ever tried stepping off a boat that is not tied to the bank?

FIG 6.32 Action and reaction

If you try to step off a boat that is not tied to the bank, you will end up in the water. The reason is that there is not one force at work but two. While a force is moving you in one direction, an equal force is moving the boat in the opposite direction.

Newton's third law of motion states that:

If an object, A, exerts a force on another object, B, then object B exerts an equal and opposite force on object A.

Another way of stating this law is 'for every action there is a reaction'.

Newton's third law tells us that:

- forces occur in pairs, which are referred to as action and reaction
- action and reaction forces are equal but occur in opposite directions.

There are lots of examples of pairs of forces to be seen in everyday life. Fig 6.33 shows an example.

FIG 6.33 When water is forced through the sprinkler jets, the action force sends it in one direction while the reaction force sends the sprinkler head in the opposite direction

1. The Ancient Greek scientist Hero is credited with inventing the first steam engine. Fig 6.34 is a model of his device.

FIG 6.34 The steam engine of Hero of Alexandria

When water is placed in the hollow sphere and heated, steam comes out of the jets causing the device to rotate.

Predict the direction that the device will rotate and explain how you know this using Newton's third law.

Fun fact

The action and reaction do not act on the same object but on different objects. Since the forces are equal and opposite, if they acted on the same object they would cancel each other out and no acceleration would be possible.

Key term

Newton's third law of motion if an object, A, exerts a force on another object, B, then object B exerts an equal and opposite force on object A

The turning effect of a force

We are learning how to:

- discuss factors that affect the moment of a force
- calculate the moment of a force.

The turning effect ⟫

A door is attached to its frame on one side by hinges.

A door does not move in the direction of the push force but turns on its hinges. This is called the turning effect or **moment of a force**. The point around which an object turns is called the **pivot** or **fulcrum**.

FIG 6.35 When a push force is applied to the door handle, the door does not move in the direction of the force but turns on its hinges

Activity 6.5

Moments in everyday life

You should work in a small group.

You will not need any equipment or materials for this activity.

Here is what you should do:

1. Discuss in your group where you use the turning effect of a force in everyday life.

2. Make a list of these examples.

The moment of a force depends both on the size of the force and also on the perpendicular distance from the pivot.

moment of a force = force (*F*) × perpendicular distance from the pivot (*d*)

The unit is the newton metre, N m. However, if the distance is measured in centimetres the moments may be expressed in N cm.

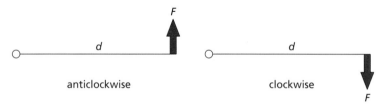

FIG 6.36 Since an object might turn in two directions around a pivot, it is sometimes necessary to state whether a moment is in an anticlockwise or clockwise direction

Worked example 6.6

What moment is created by a force of 8 N acting on a gate 1.8 m wide?

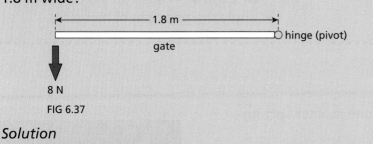

FIG 6.37

Solution

moment = 8 × 1.8 = 14.4 N m

Couples

Sometimes turning is the result of not one force but two equal forces acting in opposite directions.

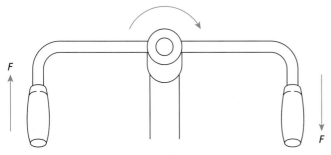

FIG 6.38 When you steer your bicycle around a bend with both hands on the handle-bars, you push with one hand and pull with the other

Forces that are equal in size and opposite in direction form a **couple** and cause rotation.

Check your understanding

1. A force of 20 N acts 5 cm from a pivot.

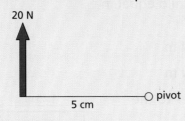

FIG 6.39

What is the moment of this force?

Fun fact

It takes more force to push open a door when its knob is at the centre.

FIG 6.40

When the knob is at the centre the distance to the hinges is only half what it would be if the knob was at the edge of the door. It takes twice the force to create the moment needed to open the door.

Key terms

moment of a force the turning effect of a force

pivot (fulcrum) the point around which an object turns

couple forces that are equal in size and opposite in direction, and cause rotation

Principle of moments

We are learning how to:

- discuss factors that affect the moment of a force
- apply the principle of moments.

Moments 〉〉〉

Sometimes there may be more than one moment acting about a pivot.

On a seesaw, one person creates an anticlockwise moment while the other creates a clockwise moment. If the moments are not equal, the seesaw will not be balanced; one side will be down and the other will be up.

FIG 6.41 There are two moments about the pivot of a seesaw

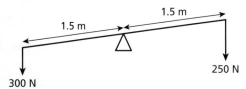

FIG 6.42 Unbalanced moments

The seesaw in Fig 6.42 is not balanced because:

anticlockwise moment = 300 × 1.5 = 450 N m

clockwise moment = 250 × 1.5 = 375 N m

There are two ways in which the seesaw can be balanced so that the seesaw is horizontal.

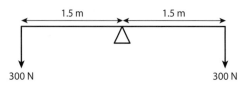

FIG 6.43 Balanced moments

The lighter child could be replaced by another child equal in weight to the heavier child.

anticlockwise moment = 300 × 1.5 = 450 N m

clockwise moment = 300 × 1.5 = 450 N m

Alternatively, the heavier child could move closer to the pivot.

anticlockwise moment = 300 × 1.25 = 375 N m

clockwise moment = 250 × 1.5 = 375 N m

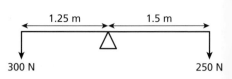

FIG 6.44 Balanced moments

The **principle of moments** states that when a system is in **equilibrium** the anticlockwise moments are equal to the clockwise moments.

In other words, there is no overall turning effect when the moments are balanced.

anticlockwise moments = clockwise moments

A system at equilibrium is stable because the effects of the forces acting on it cancel each other out.

Worked example 6.7

What force, F, is needed so that the seesaw in Fig 6.45 is balanced?

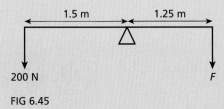

FIG 6.45

Solution

anticlockwise moment = 200 × 1.5 = 300 N m

clockwise moment = F × 1.25

When the seesaw is balanced:

clockwise moment = anticlockwise moment

$1.25F = 300$

$F = 300 \div 1.25 = 240$ N

Check your understanding

1. Fig 6.46 shows a truck.

FIG 6.46

a) In terms of moments, explain why the front of the truck is up in the air.

b) Explain what needs to be done to return it to the ground.

Fun fact

There can be more than one moment acting in the same direction about a pivot.

FIG 6.47

The seesaw in Fig 6.47 is in equilibrium because the sum of the anticlockwise moments created by the smaller children is equal to the clockwise moment created by the bigger child.

Key terms

principle of moments when a system is in equilibrium the anticlockwise moments are equal to the clockwise moments

equilibrium a system is in equilibrium when there is no overall turning effect or resultant force acting on it

Proving the principle of moments

We are learning how to:

- discuss factors that affect the moment of a force
- prove the principle of moments.

Proving the principle of moments ⟫

You can prove the principle of moments using only a ruler and some masses.

Activity 6.6

Investigating the principle of moments

Here is what you need:

- metre rule with hole drilled exactly at the centre
- 50 g mass on hanger
- 100 g mass on hanger
- stand and clamp
- nail.

Here is what you should do:

1. Place the nail in a clamp to support the metre rule.

2. Place the metre rule on the nail and make sure it is free moving.

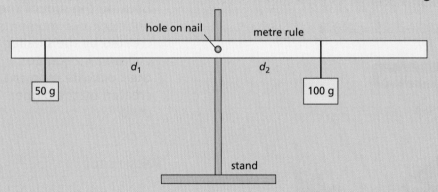

FIG 6.48

3. Copy this table.

50 g mass	d_1 (cm)	100 g mass	d_2 (cm)	$50 \times d_1$	$100 \times d_2$
50		100			
50		100			
50		100			
50		100			
50		100			
50		100			

TABLE 6.2

4. Place the 50 g mass at a point on one side of the ruler.

5. Move the 100 g mass on the other side of the ruler until you find a point where the ruler is balanced.

6. Write the values of d_1 and d_2 in your table.

7. Repeat steps 4 and 5 five times, finding new positions for the masses each time.

8. For each position, calculate the anticlockwise moment and the clockwise moment and comment on their values.

Sometimes more than one force might act on an object to produce a moment. **Parallel forces** acting either side of a pivot will each create a separate moment.

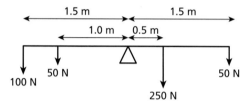

FIG 6.49 Parallel forces

total anticlockwise moments = 100 × 1.5 + 50 × 1

= 150 + 50 = 200 N m

total clockwise moments = 50 × 1.5 + 250 × 0.5

= 75 + 125 = 200 N m

In this case, the object is in equilibrium because the sum of the clockwise moments is equal to the sum of the anticlockwise moments.

Check your understanding

1. Fig 6.50 shows parallel forces acting on an object that has its centre on a pivot.

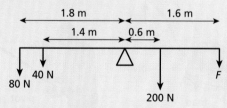

FIG 6.50

a) Calculate the anticlockwise moments acting on the object.

b) Calculate the clockwise moments acting on the object.

c) Calculate the force, F, needed to balance the moments acting around the pivot.

Fun fact

The weight of an object like a ruler is thought to act through its centre.

weight

FIG 6.51

When the centre of the ruler is placed exactly on the pivot, the ruler does not create a moment so the weight of the ruler can be ignored in calculations.

Key term

parallel forces forces that are acting in parallel directions

Levers

We are learning how to:

- discuss factors that affect the moment of a force
- describe the actions of levers in terms of moments.

What is a lever?

A **lever** is a very common simple machine in which an effort is applied at one place on a lever to overcome a load at another. The lever moves about a fixed point called the fulcrum or pivot. Both the effort and the load create moments about the pivot.

Levers may be classified into three orders on the basis of the relative positions of the effort, load and pivot.

First-order levers

In **first-order levers** the pivot lies between the effort and the load.

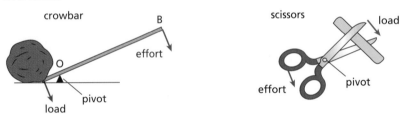

FIG 6.53 A crowbar and scissors are both examples of first-order levers

Second-order levers

In **second-order levers** the load lies between the effort and the pivot.

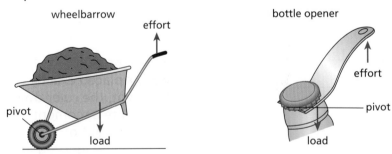

FIG 6.54 A wheelbarrow and a bottle opener are both examples of second-order levers

Third-order levers

In **third-order levers** the effort lies between the pivot and the load.

FIG 6.52 A tyre lever is used to remove a tyre from a wheel

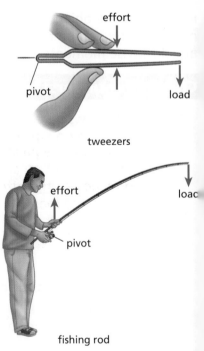

FIG 6.55 A pair of tweezers and a fishing rod are both examples of third-order levers

Activity 6.7

Different kinds of levers in the body

You might find it useful to work with a partner for this activity.

Here is what you need:

- a weight of some kind.

Here is what you should do:

The human skeleton contains examples of all three orders of lever. Carry out the following actions and decide between you which order of lever is involved. To do this you will have to think not only about the parts of the body that move, but also where muscles apply the effort.

1. Rise up on the balls of your feet so your heels are off the ground. Which muscles are contracted? Where are the effort, load and pivot?

2. Pick up a weight with your hand and hold your arm out so it is bent at the elbow. Which muscles are contracted? Where are the effort, load and pivot?

3. Tilt your head forwards so you are looking at the ground. Which muscles are contracted? Where are the effort, load and pivot?

Fun fact

In each class of lever the effort and the load both create a moment about the pivot.

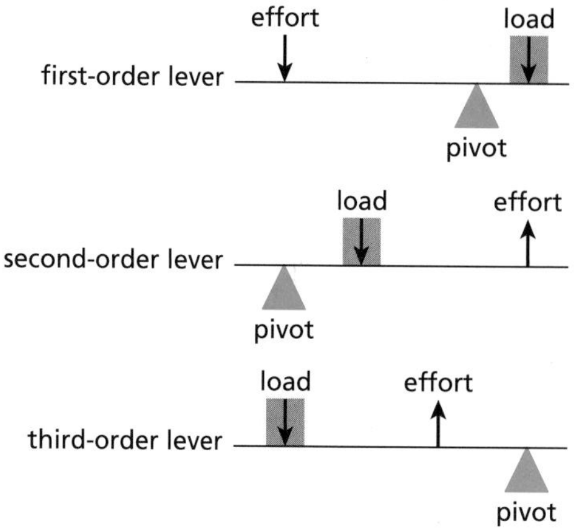

FIG 6.57

Check your understanding

1. Fig 6.56 shows a claw hammer being used as a lever to remove a nail from wood.

   a) Draw a diagram of this and mark the pivot, and the position and direction of the effort and of the load.

   b) What class of lever is the hammer when used in this way?

FIG 6.56

Key terms

lever very common simple machine in which an effort is applied at one place to overcome a load at another

first-order levers levers where the pivot lies between the effort and the load

second-order levers levers where the load lies between the effort and the pivot

third-order levers levers where the effort lies between the pivot and the load

Calculations on levers

We are learning how to:

- discuss factors that affect the moment of a force
- carry out calculations on levers.

Lever calculations 〉〉〉

The principle of moments states that when a body is in equilibrium, the sum of the clockwise moments about any point is equal to the sum of the anticlockwise moments. You can apply this principle to levers.

The boulder in Fig 6.58 exerts a force of 1200 N downwards due to its weight. The boulder creates an anticlockwise moment of 1200 × 10 = 12 000 N cm about the pivot. When an effort force is applied to the other end of the crowbar, it will create a clockwise moment about the pivot.

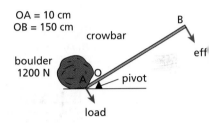

FIG 6.58 Using a crowbar to raise a boulder

As the boulder just begins to move you can say, taking moments about the pivot, that:

clockwise moment = anticlockwise moment

effort × 150 = 1200 × 10

$$\text{effort} = \frac{12\,000}{150} = 80 \text{ N}$$

The crowbar is acting as a **force multiplier** because it is increasing the effort force.

Worked example 6.8

A gardener has filled a wheelbarrow with soil.

Use the information in the diagram to calculate the effort needed to raise the handles of the wheelbarrow.

Solution

clockwise moment = effort × (0.9 + 0.3) = effort × 1.2 N m

anticlockwise moment = 400 × 0.3 = 120 N m

When the handles of the wheelbarrow just start to move:

effort × 1.2 N m = 120 N m

$$\text{effort} = \frac{120}{1.2} = 100 \text{ N}$$

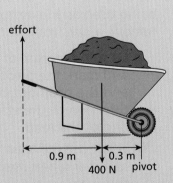

FIG 6.59

The wheelbarrow acts as a force multiplier because it allows the load to be lifted with a smaller effort. However, levers do not always act as force multipliers.

Worked example 6.9

Fig 6.60 shows a fish being raised on an angler's fishing rod.

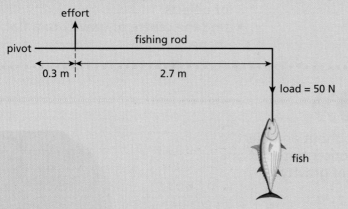

FIG 6.60

a) Use the information in the diagram to calculate the effort needed to raise the fish.

b) Explain why the fishing rod is not a force multiplier but is a distance multiplier.

Solution

a) 　　　　clockwise moment = 50 × (2.7 + 0.3) = 150 N m

　　　　anticlockwise moment = effort × 0.3 N m

　When the fishing rod just starts to move upwards:

　　　　　effort × 0.3 = 150 N

$$\text{effort} = \frac{150}{0.3} = 500 \text{ N}$$

b) The fishing rod is not a force multiplier because the effort needed is greater than the load. The fishing rod is a **distance multiplier** because the distance moved by the load is greater than the distance moved by the effort.

Fun fact

A lever can be a force multiplier or a distance multiplier but it cannot be both.

Key terms

force multiplier lever that increases the effort force (a small force is used to create a large force)

distance multiplier lever where distance moved by the load is greater than the distance moved by the effort

Check your understanding

1. Fig 6.61 shows a screwdriver being used to open a can of paint.

a) The screwdriver is acting as a simple machine. Name this machine.

b) At which point on the diagram is the pivot around which the screwdriver turns?

c) What is the moment of the screwdriver about the edge of the can?

d) If an effort of 25 N is just enough to open the can, what force, *F*, is needed to raise the lid?

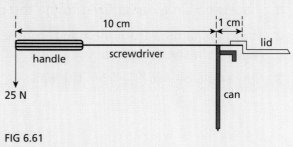

FIG 6.61

Centre of gravity

We are learning how to:

- discuss factors that affect the stability of objects
- find the centre of gravity of a flat shape.

Matter and the centre of gravity ⟩⟩

Although matter is distributed throughout an object, it behaves as if its whole weight was concentrated at one point. This point is called the **centre of gravity**.

FIG 6.62

FIG 6.63 If an earring is suspended in such a way that it is able to move, it will always hang with its centre of gravity directly below the point of attachment

If you place a support exactly at the centre of a ruler, it will remain horizontal (the weight is acting through the support therefore there is no clockwise or anticlockwise moment), but if you move the support away from the centre, the ruler will turn as the weight now creates a moment.

Activity 6.8

Finding the centre of gravity of a lamina

Here is what you need:

- stand and clamp
- nail
- irregularly-shaped lamina with two holes
- plumb line (string with weight at one end)
- pin.

Here is what you should do:

1. Place a nail in a clamp fixed to the top of a stand.

2. Hang the lamina from the nail through one of the holes (A in the diagram).

3. Suspend a plumb line from the nail.

4. Draw a line AB on the lamina where the plumb line hangs.

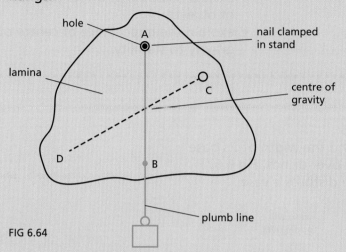

FIG 6.64

5. Repeat steps 2 to 4 but this time hang the lamina through the other hole (C in the diagram).

6. Locate the centre of gravity of the lamina where the two lines intersect.

7. Try to balance the lamina on a pivot at its centre of gravity.

Check your understanding

1. Fig 6.65 shows what happens when a car engine is raised on a steel cable.

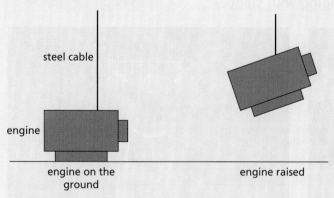

FIG 6.65

Explain why the engine twists when it is raised.

Fun fact

The centre of gravity of a regular shape is at its geometric centre.

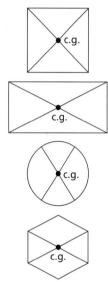

FIG 6.66

You can find the centre of gravity of these shapes by drawing diagonals, or in the case of a circle by drawing two diameters.

Key term

centre of gravity point at which whole weight of an object can be considered to be concentrated

Stability

We are learning how to:

- discuss factors that affect the stability of objects
- explain the importance of centre of gravity to stability.

Keeping stable ⟫

The position of its centre of gravity and the width of its base determine whether an object will fall over or not. Fig 6.67 shows what could happen if someone disturbs a vase.

vase will return to its original position

vase will topple over

vase | c.g.

FIG 6.67 What could happen if someone disturbs a vase

Initially the centre of gravity of the vase acts through the middle of its base. When the vase is disturbed two things might happen:

- Provided the centre of gravity remains above the base, the vase will return to its original position.

- If the centre of gravity moves outside the base, the vase will topple over.

Your centre of gravity is near the centre of your body. You can make yourself more **stable** by changing your stance.

Key term

stable unlikely to topple over

FIG 6.68 People who practise martial arts crouch forwards and move their legs apart to lower their centre of gravity and widen their base so that they are more difficult to push over

FIG 6.69 When a weight lifter raises a weight above her head, the combined centre of gravity of her body plus the weight is much higher than the centre of gravity of her body, so, to compensate for the loss of stability, she spreads her legs to increase the size of her base

Activity 6.9

Investigating the stability of a measuring cylinder

Here is what you need:

- measuring cylinder
- non-slip surface such as a cardboard drinks mat
- ruler
- water.

Here is what you should do:

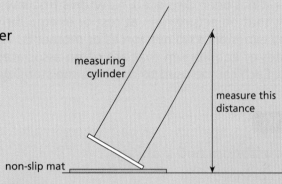

1. Place an empty measuring cylinder on a non-slip surface.

2. Pull gently on the top of the measuring cylinder until you reach the point where if you let it go, it would tip over.

3. Measure the height of the top of the measuring cylinder from the top of the table.

FIG 6.70

4. Place 50 cm³ of water in the measuring cylinder and repeat steps 2 and 3.

5. Place 100 cm³ of water in the measuring cylinder and repeat steps 2 and 3.

6. What effect does putting water in the measuring cylinder have on its stability?

Check your understanding

1. Fig 6.71 shows four vases, A, B, C and D.

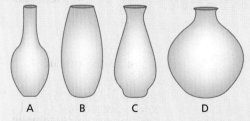

FIG 6.71

a) Which of these vases will be easiest to knock over? Explain your answer.

b) If the vase you chose in a) was filled with water, would its stability: increase, remain the same or decrease? Explain your answer.

Fun fact

In Pisa, Italy, there is a tower that leans over because its foundations are weak on one side.

FIG 6.72 Leaning Tower of Pisa

If the centre of gravity of the tower ever moves outside its base the tower will topple over.

Equilibrium

We are learning how to:

- discuss factors that affect the stability of objects
- identify three states of equilibrium.

States of equilibrium 》》》

Stability is the ability of an object to return to its rest position after it has been displaced. Newton's first law of motion states that objects remain at rest or in equilibrium provided they experience no net forces or moments. There are three states of equilibrium that are often associated with stability. Each can be used to describe the stability of an object.

Activity 6.10

States of equilibrium and stability

Here is what you need:

- marble
- large evaporating basin with round bottom.

Here is what you should do:

1. Place a marble on the table in front of you.
2. Move the marble to a position a centimetre away and release it.
3. Does the marble move or not?
4. Does the marble move back to its original position?
5. Place an evaporating basin the correct way up on the table.
6. Put the marble in the centre of the basin.
7. Move the marble to a position a centimetre away and release it.
8. Does the marble move or not?
9. Does the marble move back to its original position?
10. Now turn the evaporating basin upside down on the table.
11. Put the marble at the top of the basin.
12. Move the marble to a position a centimetre away and release it.
13. Does the marble move or not?
14. Does the marble move back to its original position?

If you place a marble on a flat surface and then move it to a new position, it will remain in the new position. The centre of gravity remains the same height above the surface.

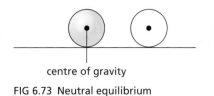

centre of gravity

FIG 6.73 Neutral equilibrium

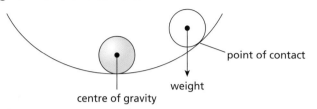

point of contact

weight

centre of gravity

FIG 6.74 Stable equilibrium

If the marble is placed on a surface that curves upwards and is then moved to a new position, it does not remain in this new position. The centre of gravity rises when it is displaced. It rolls back to its original position because the weight of the ball has a moment about the point of contact with the surface.

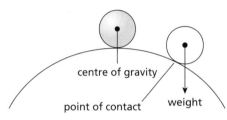

centre of gravity

point of contact

weight

FIG 6.75 Unstable equilibrium

If the marble is placed on a surface that curves downwards and is then moved to a new position, it neither remains in this new position nor rolls back to its original position. Once again, the centre of gravity has a moment about the point of contact but in this case it takes the marble further away.

Check your understanding

1. Fig 6.76 shows a roller coaster. The coaster breaks down when the train is in the position shown and the car has no brakes.

   a) Where will the train come to rest?

   b) Explain your answer in terms of stability and equilibrium.

FIG 6.76

Fun fact

You can balance a needle on its point using the apparatus below.

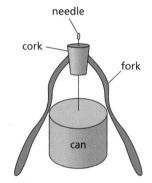

needle

cork

fork

can

FIG 6.77

The centre of gravity is vertically below the point of contact and the equilibrium is therefore stable.

Key term

stability the ability of an object to return to its rest position after it has been displaced

Review of Motion

- Speed is the rate at which an object moves from one point to another. It is measured in metres per second, m/s, or kilometres per hour, km/h. The equation for speed is:

$$\text{speed (m/s)} = \frac{\text{distance (m)}}{\text{time (s)}}$$

- A distance–time graph shows distance on the vertical or y-axis and time on the horizontal or x-axis. The speed of an object is given by the slope or gradient of a distance–time graph.

- Displacement is the distance an object moves in a particular direction and is measured in the same units as distance – for example, metres, m.

- Velocity is the speed an object travels in a particular direction and is measured in the same units – for example, metres/second, m/s. The equation for velocity is:

$$\text{velocity (m/s)} = \frac{\text{displacement (m)}}{\text{time (s)}}$$

- Acceleration is the rate at which velocity changes over time. It is a result of unbalanced forces acting on an object. Acceleration is measured in metres per second per second, m/s^2. The equation for acceleration is:

$$\text{acceleration (m/s}^2\text{)} = \frac{\text{change in velocity (m/s)}}{\text{time (s)}}$$

- Inertia is the resistance of an object to change its state of motion. Objects with greater mass have greater inertia.

- Momentum is the product of an object's mass and its velocity. The unit of momentum is the kilogram metre per second, kg m/s.

$$\text{momentum (kg m/s)} = \text{mass (kg)} \times \text{velocity (m/s)}$$

- Objects with greater mass have greater momentum. Objects with greater velocity have greater momentum.

- Newton proposed three laws of motion:

  1. A body will remain in a state of rest or uniform motion in a straight line unless it is acted on by an external force.

  2. When a force acts on an object, it will accelerate in the direction of the force. The amount of acceleration is directly proportional to the force applied and inversely proportional to the mass of the object.

  3. If an object, A, exerts a force on another object, B, then object B exerts an equal and opposite force on object A.

- When a force has a turning effect this is called a moment. A moment can be anticlockwise or clockwise.

  moment (N m) = force (N) × perpendicular distance from pivot (m)

  When two equal but opposite forces act about the same point, a couple is formed and this causes rotation.

- The principle of moments states that when a system is in equilibrium the anticlockwise moments are equal to the clockwise moments.

  anticlockwise moments = clockwise moments

- Levers are simple machines in which effort and load forces both create moments about a common pivot.

  - In a first-order lever the pivot is located between the effort and the load.

  - In a second-order lever the load is located between the effort and the pivot.

  - In a third-order lever the effort is located between the pivot and the load.

- The centre of gravity of an object is a point at which all of its weight is considered to be concentrated.

- If an object is freely suspended, it always hangs with its centre of gravity directly below the point at which it is attached.

- If an object is tilted so that its centre of gravity is outside its base, it will topple over.

- Objects that are most stable are those that have a low centre of gravity and a broad base.

- An object might be in neutral equilibrium, stable equilibrium or unstable equilibrium depending on its position.

Review questions on Motion

1. Fig 6.RQ.1 shows a lever being used to raise a heavy weight.

   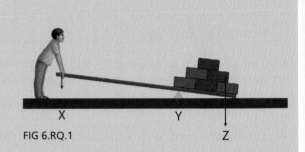

   FIG 6.RQ.1

   a) Choose from the following words to identify X, Y and Z.

   pivot　　　　load　　　　effort

   b) Is the lever acting as a force multiplier or a distance multiplier?

   c) Should the man move Y closer to X or closer to Z in order to reduce the amount of force he needs to exert?

2. Fig 6.RQ.2 shows three possible states of equilibrium.

   a)

   b)

   c)

   FIG 6.RQ.2

   Describe the type of equilibrium represented by each part of the diagram.

3. State whether each of the following is a first-order, second-order or third-order lever.

   a)

   FIG 6.RQ.3

   b)

   FIG 6.RQ.4

   c)

   FIG 6.RQ.5

4. A 'speed camera' is able to detect the speed of a car. The lines on the road are exactly 2 m apart. The camera takes two photographs, the second exactly 0.5 s after the first.

   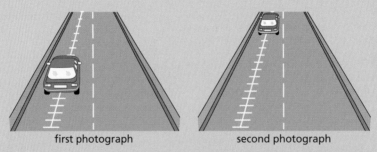

   first photograph　　　　second photograph

   FIG 6.RQ.6

   a) The speed limit on this road is 60 km/h. What is this speed in m/s?

   b) How far did the car travel between the first and second pictures?

   c) Calculate the speed of the car and decide if it was exceeding the speed limit.

5. Fig 6.RQ.7 shows how the velocity of a car changes over a short journey.

a) During which period, A, B or C, is the car:

   i) slowing down?

   ii) speeding up?

   iii) travelling at a constant velocity?

b) What is the fastest velocity at which the car travels? Give this in m/s and in km/hour.

c) What is the acceleration of the car in the first 50 seconds of the journey?

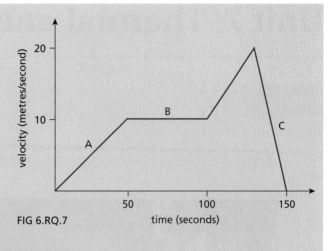

FIG 6.RQ.7

6. Kyle is tightening the wheel nuts on his bicycle wheel using a spanner.

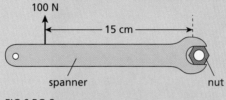

FIG 6.RQ.8

a) Is the spanner acting as a force multiplier or a distance multiplier? Explain this.

b) Calculate the size of the moment on the nut and state its direction.

c) Kyle has a hollow pipe that fits over the end of the spanner.

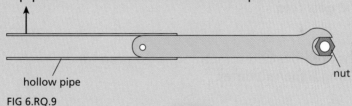

FIG 6.RQ.9

Explain why using the hollow pipe allows him to exert a greater moment on the nut.

7. Fig 6.RQ.10 shows three solid shapes. The centre of gravity is marked on each of them.

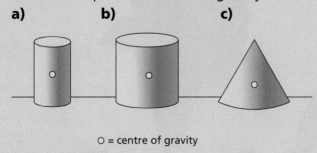

O = centre of gravity

FIG 6.RQ.10

With the help of suitable diagrams show which is least stable and which is most stable.

Unit 7: Thermal energy

Introduction 》》

Heat

Heat is a form of energy. You use heat in lots of different ways.

FIG 7.1 Heat is used for cooking our food

Heat is used for cooking food, heating water and warming our homes when it gets cold.

Temperature

To find out how hot or how cold something is, you can take its temperature using a thermometer.

FIG 7.2 Doctors and nurses sometimes measure a person's body temperature because an increase in normal body temperature might indicate illness

Heat transfer

The uses you make of heat energy involve transferring it from one place to another.

FIG 7.3 To cook food, heat must be transferred through the bottom of a pan

Heat must be transferred from the burning gas through the bottom of the pan to the food.

FIG 7.4 To warm the Earth, heat must be transferred across space from the Sun

By the end of this unit you will appreciate that there are three different methods of heat transfer.

> **Challenge**
>
> Heat transfer is often very useful, but not always. Can you think of any examples where you might want to prevent heat transfer?

Heat and temperature

We are learning how to:

- distinguish between temperature and heat
- use different scales to measure temperature.

What are heat and temperature? »»

Thermal energy is often called heat energy or **heat**. The terms heat and **temperature** are connected but they do not mean the same thing.

Heat is a form of energy. Like all energy, it is measured in joules. Heat energy flows from a hotter body to a colder body.

Temperature is a measure of how hot or how cold something is. When a body gains heat energy, its temperature rises, and when it loses heat energy, its temperature falls.

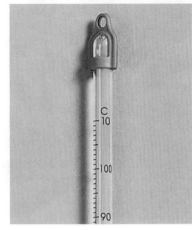

FIG 7.5 Temperature is expressed in degrees Celsius (symbol °C)

Activity 7.1

Heat transfer

Here is what you need:

- two beakers
- hot water, but not too hot to place your finger in
- iced water.

Here is what you should do:

1. Three-quarter fill a beaker with hot water.
2. Three-quarter fill a beaker with iced water.
3. Place your finger into each beaker in turn and note that the water is hot in one and cold in the other.
4. Leave the beakers to stand on the table throughout the lesson.
5. Near the end of the lesson place your finger into each beaker in turn.
6. Is the difference between hot and cold as great as it was at the start of the lesson?
7. What has happened to the water in each of the beakers?

When objects are different temperatures there is a temperature gradient between them. Heat energy is lost by the hotter object and absorbed by the colder object until their temperatures are equal.

Celsius scale

Temperature is measured using a **thermometer**. The units of temperature most commonly used are **degrees Celsius**. This unit has the symbol °C.

The Celsius scale is also sometimes called the **centigrade** scale. The Celsius scale was devised by the Swedish astronomer Anders Celsius in the eighteenth century.

Kelvin scale

Although the Celsius scale is widely used in science, it has one drawback. The melting point and boiling point of some substances are below 0 °C and therefore must be written as negative values.

In order to avoid this problem a new scale was devised by Lord Kelvin. This scale started at the lowest possible temperature, which is −273.16 °C. This is absolute zero. To make conversion between the two scales easier, the start of the **kelvin** scale, which is 0 K, is taken to be −273 °C.

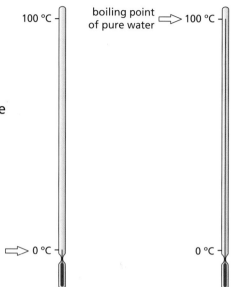

FIG 7.6 On the Celsius scale, pure water freezes at 0 °C and it boils at 100 °C, at normal atmospheric pressure (these two temperatures are sometimes called fixed points)

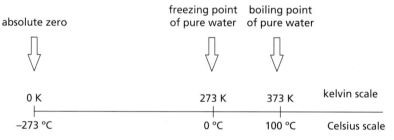

FIG 7.7 Kelvin and Celsius scales

Notice that the unit is the kelvin and not the degree kelvin, and it is written as K and not °K. The kelvin is the SI unit of temperature.

Check your understanding

Use the words 'heat' or 'temperature' to complete each of the following sentences.

1. When a body receives .... energy its .... increases.

2. .... is a form of energy while .... is a measure of how hot or cold a body is.

3. When an object is cooled its .... falls because it loses ....

4. The .... of a pond increases during the day because it receives .... from the Sun.

Key terms

thermal energy a form of energy

heat a form of energy

temperature a measure of how hot or how cold something is

thermometer an instrument used to measure temperature

degree Celsius a unit of temperature

centigrade a unit of temperature

kelvin a unit of temperature

Thermometers

We are learning how to:

- distinguish between temperature and heat
- use a thermometer to measure temperature.

Measuring temperature ⟫

The thermometers most commonly used in the laboratory and elsewhere are called liquid-in-glass thermometers. They consist of a sealed length of capillary tube with a bulb at one end.

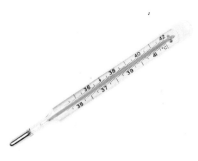

FIG 7.8 There are two liquids commonly used in these thermometers: alcohol (ethanol) and mercury

Care must be taken when reading liquid-in-glass thermometers to obtain accurate readings.

Reading a thermometer accurately

When a liquid is placed in a narrow tube, the surface or **meniscus** is not flat but curved.

The reading on an alcohol thermometer is always taken from the position of the bottom of the meniscus.

The reading on a mercury thermometer is always taken from the position of the top of the meniscus.

Notice that when you read a thermometer, your eye should be level with the top of the liquid.

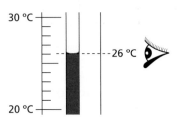

FIG 7.9 The meniscus formed by a thread of alcohol is lower at the centre than at the sides

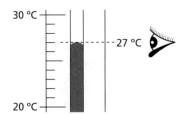

FIG 7.10 The meniscus formed by a thread of mercury is higher at the centre than at the sides

Activity 7.2

Reading a thermometer accurately

Here is what you need:

- thermometer
- five beakers containing water at different temperatures.

 SAFETY

Take care when using hot water. Follow local regulations.

Here is what you should do:

1. Place the thermometer into a beaker containing water.
2. Leave it for a few minutes.
3. Record the temperature on the thermometer.
4. Repeat steps 1 to 3 for beakers containing water at different temperatures.

Check your understanding

1. What is the reading on each of the following thermometers to the nearest half of a degree Celsius?

a)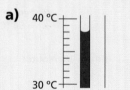

b)

c)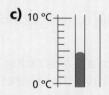

d)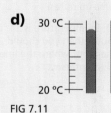

e)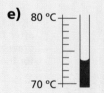

f)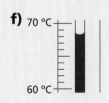

FIG 7.11

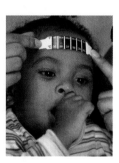

FIG 7.12 A simple thermocolour thermometer can be used to show the temperature in a room or in a device such as a refrigerator, or it can be placed on the forehead of a person to measure body temperature

Key term

meniscus surface of a liquid

Cooling graphs

We are learning how to:

- distinguish between temperature and heat
- interpret and draw cooling graphs.

Cooling graphs »»

When a warm object is left in a room it will gradually cool down until the temperature is the same as room temperature.

You can draw a **cooling curve** similar to this for a sample of hot water as it cools down by measuring its temperature every two minutes and using the data to plot a graph of temperature against time. Before you start taking measurements, you will need to draw a table like this for your results.

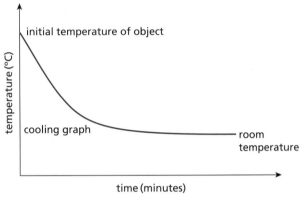

FIG 7.13 How the temperature of the object would change as it cools down

Temperature (°C)	Time (minutes)
	0
	2
	4

TABLE 7.1

You will need to plot each point in the correct position on the graph.

The points that you obtain will form a curve rather than a straight line. Do not try to draw a curve that passes through every point.

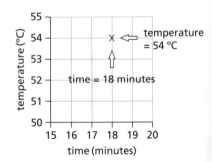

FIG 7.14 If the temperature is 54 °C after 18 minutes then you should draw X at the point where the lines for these values intersect

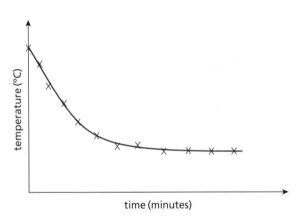

FIG 7.15 Draw a smooth curve that goes through the majority of the points and represents the pattern shown by the data

Activity 7.3

Cooling graph for water

Here is what you need:

- thermometer
- beaker containing water at about 70 °C
- graph paper.

 SAFETY

Take care when using hot water. Follow local regulations.

Here is what you should do:

1. Draw a table to record your results.
2. Place the thermometer into a beaker containing water.
3. Leave it for a few minutes.
4. Record the initial temperature of the water.
5. Record the temperature of the water every two minutes until there is no change in its temperature for two consecutive readings.
6. Plot a graph of temperature on the vertical or *y*-axis against time on the horizontal or *x*-axis.
7. Draw the curve of best fit through your plots.
8. Use your curve to find:
   a) the final temperature of the water
   b) the time taken for the water to reach this temperature.

> **Fun fact**
>
> Equal masses of liquid at the same temperature do not cool down at the same rate.
>
>
>
> 100 g water   100 g olive oil
>
> FIG 7.16 100 g of olive oil will cool down more quickly than 100 g of water

Check your understanding

1. Briefly describe how you would obtain a cooling graph for a liquid.

2. Plot a cooling graph from this data, which shows the cooling of a cup of coffee:

Time (minutes)	0	1	2	3	4	5	6	7
Temp. (°C)	75	66	60	55	52	50	49	48

TABLE 7.2

Key term

cooling curve graph that shows how the temperature falls as cooling occurs

Heat transfer – conduction

We are learning how to:

- compare types of heat transfer
- describe conduction as the process by which heat is transferred through solids.

Heat transfer ⟩⟩⟩

For heat to be transferred there needs to be a difference in temperature between two points. There are three different methods of **heat transfer**:

- **conduction** – this is the main process by which heat is transferred through solids

- **convection** – this is the main process by which heat is transferred through liquids and gases

- **radiation** – this is the process by which heat can be transferred across open spaces, including the vacuum of outer space.

In real situations, heat is often transferred by a combination of these processes.

FIG 7.17 A log fire heats a room by convection and radiation

Conduction

In solids, the particles are held in fixed positions. They cannot move position but they do vibrate.

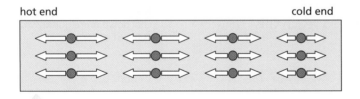

hot end   cold end

FIG 7.18 Conduction in a solid

When a solid is heated, the particles vibrate more energetically. The particles jostle neighbouring particles and in this way movement energy is passed through the solid. This process is called conduction. All solids conduct heat to some extent but some solids are much better **heat conductors** than others.

Activity 7.4

Do all solids conduct heat energy at the same rate?

Here is what you need:

- rods of metals and non-metals (such as copper, iron, glass, wood)
- candle wax
- boiling water
- large beaker
- cardboard
- small beaker.

> ⚠️ **SAFETY**
> Take care when heating. Follow local regulations.

Here is what you should do:

1. Melt candle wax in a small beaker using an electric heater.

2. Dip one end of each rod in the wax so that it is covered in the wax.

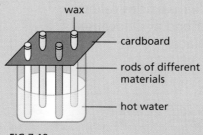
FIG 7.19

3. Make four holes in a square of cardboard. Make the holes just big enough to push the four rods through.

4. Put the rods in the water so the wax-coated ends are out of the water.

5. On which rod did the wax melt first?

6. On which rod did the wax melt last?

7. Which material is the best conductor of heat?

8. Which material is the poorest conductor of heat?

All metals are good conductors of heat while most non-metals are poor conductors. Poor conductors of heat are called **thermal insulators** and include glass, plastics, wood, water and air.

Check your understanding

1. Explain why a toasting fork is made of metal but has a wooden handle.

FIG 7.20

Fun fact

Although diamonds are non-metals, they are the best heat-conducting solids known.

FIG 7.21 Diamond conducts heat five times better than copper

Key terms

heat transfer transfer of heat from one place to another

conduction the main process by which heat is transferred through solids

convection the main process by which heat is transferred through liquids and gases

radiation the main process by which heat is transferred through a vacuum such as space

heat conductors objects that transfer heat energy easily

thermal insulators objects that do not transfer heat energy easily

Metals as conductors of heat

We are learning how to:

- compare types of heat transfer
- explain why metals are good heat conductors in terms of their structure.

Why are metals good conductors? »»

The reason why **metals** are good conductors of heat can be explained by considering their structure.

A metal consists of a framework of tiny particles. Between these particles there are even smaller particles called electrons. These electrons are described as delocalised because they are not held in one place.

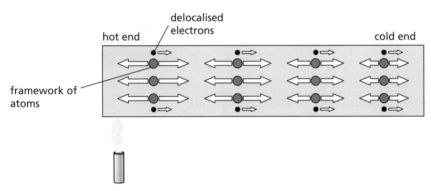

FIG 7.22 Metals have mobile electrons

When a metal is heated the particles vibrate more energetically, just like the particles of any solid but, in addition to this, heating increases the movement energy of the delocalised electrons. The delocalised electrons move quickly and are able to transfer energy through the metal very quickly.

Activity 7.5

Do all metals conduct heat energy equally well?

Here is what you need:

- conduction wheel (Fig 7.23) or strips of four different metals of equal length
- tripod
- small beaker
- candle wax
- four paperclips
- heat source.

SAFETY

Take care when heating. Follow local regulations.

Here is what you should do:

1. Melt some candle wax in a small beaker.

2. Put a small amount of molten candle wax on the end of the underside of each metal strip in turn and hold a paperclip to it until the wax hardens.

3. When the metal strip is placed the right way up, the paperclip should hang down from it.

4. Place the wheel on a tripod and heat the wheel at the centre.

5. Record the time taken for the paperclip to fall from each metal strip. Write your answers in a table like this.

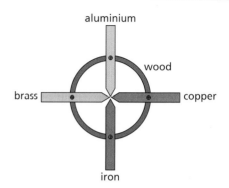

FIG 7.23

Metal	Time taken for paperclip to fall (s)

TABLE 7.3

6. State the order in which the metals conduct heat, starting with the best conductor.

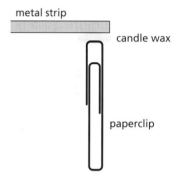

FIG 7.24

Check your understanding

1. Some results for the activity described above are given in the table.

Metal	Time taken for paperclip to fall (s)
aluminium	45
brass	83
copper	26
iron	125

TABLE 7.4

a) How can you decide which metal is the best conductor?

b) State the order in which these metals conduct heat, starting with the best conductor.

c) Chromium is a better conductor than iron but not as good as brass. Suggest the time it would have taken for a paperclip attached by wax to fall from a strip of chromium.

Fun fact

Some cooks prefer using pans that have copper bottoms.

FIG 7.25 Copper is a better conductor of heat than aluminium or stainless steel so heat is transferred to the food more quickly

Key term

metal a type of material with delocalised electrons

183

Heat transfer – convection

We are learning how to:

- compare types of heat transfer
- describe convection as the main process by which heat is transferred through liquids and gases.

Convection ⟫

The particles in liquids and gases are too far apart for conduction to take place effectively. Heat is mainly transferred through liquids and gases by another process called convection.

When the particles in a liquid or a gas are heated, they move about more quickly. The particles spread out so they are further apart from each other. The volume of a liquid increases a small amount while the volume of a gas increases by a large amount.

Since the density of a substance is equal to its mass divided by its volume, it follows that when the volume of a liquid or gas increases, its density decreases. This decrease in density is the cause of convection. The less dense substance rises above the more dense substance.

Convection in liquids

It is possible to observe convection taking place in water by introducing a coloured chemical or dye to it.

Activity 7.6

Convection in water

Here is what you need:

- beaker
- tripod
- drinking straw
- small crystal of potassium manganate(VII) or dye
- small candle of other heat source.

 SAFETY

Take care when heating. Do not touch potassium manganate(VII) with bare hands. Follow local regulations.

cold water

crystal of potassium manganate(VII)

FIG 7.26

Here is what you should do:

1. Place cold water into the beaker until it is almost full and place it on a tripod.

2. Stand the drinking straw near the edge of the beaker and carefully drop a small crystal of potassium manganate(VII) down the straw so it sits in the corner of the beaker.

3. Gently warm the water around the crystal of potassium manganate(VII) and observe how the purple colour of this chemical passes through the water.

4. Continue careful heating until all of the water is purple.

5. Draw a diagram to show how the colour passes through the water in the beaker.

The particles responsible for the colour are carried by the water as it moves.

When the water around a coloured crystal at the bottom of the beaker is heated, it becomes less dense and rises, carrying some of the coloured particles with it. Cooler water from the top of the beaker falls down to replace it. Overall, the water rises as it gets warm and falls down as it cools. This movement is called a **convection current**.

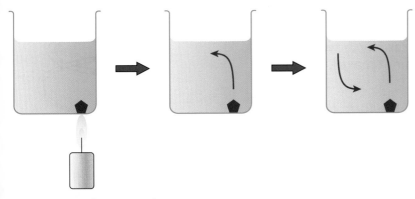

FIG 7.27 Convection currents in water

Fun fact

Convection currents occur on a massive scale in the oceans and in the atmosphere, and are an important factor in determining climate. Differences in temperature at different points in the oceans and the atmosphere result in the formation of convection currents.

In the oceans, convection currents help to circulate nutrients from the ocean floor into shallow water, where they promote the growth of organisms.

Check your understanding

1. With the help of a suitable diagram, explain how heat is transferred through water in a heated pan.

2. Describe what convection currents you would expect to notice in the air in a kitchen when there is a hot cooking hob at one side of the kitchen.

Key term

convection current
movement of particles of a liquid or gas as a result of convection

Convection in gases

We are learning how to:

- compare types of heat transfer
- explain convection in gases in terms of changes in density.

Hot air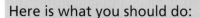

Convection takes place in gases in exactly the same way as in liquids.

Birds of prey know all about convection currents. They spread their wings and rise up on the air that has been warmed by the land.

FIG 7.28 Birds of prey can rise to great heights without having to use much energy

Activity 7.7

To show that warm air rises

Here is what you need:

- square of thin card
- scissors
- needle
- cotton
- small candle.

⚠️ **SAFETY**
Take care when heating. Follow local regulations.

Here is what you should do:

1. Draw a snake on a piece of card by drawing a spiral line out from the centre. Do not make the snake too thin.

2. Cut out your snake so it is in the form of a spiral.

3. Thread a piece of cotton through the head of your snake. Tie a big knot at one end to stop the cotton falling through the hole and tie the other end to the end of a pencil.

4. Hold your snake above a small candle flame.

⚠️ **SAFETY**
Do not place the snake too near the flame or it will catch alight and burn.

5. Describe and explain what happens to your snake.

FIG 7.29

It is important to appreciate that during convection it is not heat energy that is rising but the heated liquid or gas. The heat energy increases the movement energy of the particles in the liquid or gas. As the movement energy increases, the density decreases and the less dense substance moves above the more dense substance.

In the atmosphere, convection currents are responsible for winds. The Sun does not heat the atmosphere directly. The Sun heats the surface of the Earth and this, in turn, heats the air above it. When the air above the Earth's surface is heated it expands, its density decreases and it rises, creating an area of low pressure. Cooler, denser air moves in from surrounding areas of higher pressure to replace the rising air.

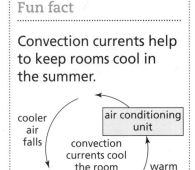

FIG 7.31 Modern factories have ventilation fans in their roofs to extract the hot air that rises inside the factory

FIG 7.30 You can see convection in a gas by observing a fire: smoke particles from the fire rise because they are carried upwards by the hot air

Check your understanding

1. A smoke box consists of a box that has two chimneys. A candle is burned under one chimney while smoke from smouldering wooden splints is introduced at the other. The smoke box has a glass front so the movement of smoke can be observed.

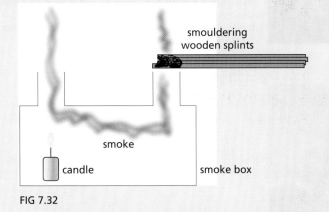

FIG 7.32

a) Explain why smoke from the smouldering wooden splints is drawn into the box.

b) Would the same thing happen if the candle was not burning? Explain your answer.

Fun fact

Convection currents help to keep rooms cool in the summer.

cooler air falls

air conditioning unit

convection currents cool the room

warm air rises

FIG 7.33

Warm air rises and passes through the air conditioning unit. The cooler air falls, pushing the warm air upwards.

Heat transfer – radiation

We are learning how to:

- compare types of heat transfer
- describe radiation as the process by which heat is transferred across a vacuum.

Radiation >>>

The Earth and the other planets are separated from the Sun by the vacuum of space. A vacuum contains nothing; no solids, liquids or gases. How does heat therefore travel from the Sun to the Earth and the other planets? There is a third way in which thermal energy can be transferred called radiation.

Heat radiation consists of infrared waves that can travel through a vacuum in much the same way as visible light. Heat radiation is not limited to space. There are many examples of devices on Earth that emit heat radiation.

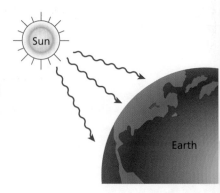

FIG 7.34 Heat radiation travels through space to Earth

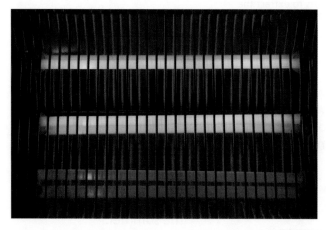

FIG 7.35 An electric fire emits a combination of visible light, which you can see, and heat radiation, which you can feel (the shiny reflector behind the heating element helps to direct the heat radiation into a room)

FIG 7.36 Houses in places that get lots of sunshine are often painted in bright colours (the bright colours reflect more of the sunlight than dark colours so the inside of the house is kept cooler)

Tinted glass contains particles of iron that absorb heat radiation. This reduces the amount of heat radiation passing through the window so the inside of the car stays cooler.

FIG 7.37 Many cars have tinted windows

Activity 7.8

Reducing heat radiation

You will not need any equipment or materials for this activity.

Here is what you should do:

Some different ways of reducing the effect of heat radiation are described in the lesson.

1. Carry out research into some other ways of reducing the effects of heat radiation.

2. Makes some notes and be prepared to share what you have found out in a class discussion.

Check your understanding

1. How do you know that heat does not travel from the Sun to the Earth by conduction or convection?

2. In what form is heat radiation transferred?

3. Why does an electric fire have a shiny metal plate behind the heating element?

4. How can the human body detect heat radiation?

Fun fact

When it is dark, you cannot see the reflected light from objects, but thermal imaging binoculars detect the heat radiation that they emit.

FIG 7.38 'Seeing' in the dark

Radiation and absorption of different surfaces

We are learning how to:

- compare types of heat transfer
- identify good and poor radiators of heat.

Emitting and absorbing radiation ⟩⟩

Objects can both **emit** and **absorb** heat radiation.

31.6

FIG 7.39 The heat radiation that is continually emitted by a person makes it possible to 'see' them in the dark using a device that detects heat

FIG 7.40 The water in a swimming pool warms up when the Sun shines on it for a few hours

Activity 7.9

To investigate if different surfaces absorb heat radiation equally well

Here is what you need:

- two cans of equal size: one shiny and the other painted matt black
- measuring cylinder
- two thermometers.

Here is what you should do;

1. Using a measuring cylinder, fill the two cans with equal amounts of cold water from the same source.

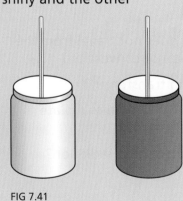

FIG 7.41

2. Place a thermometer in each can and measure the temperature of the water it contains.

3. Write the temperatures in a table.

4. Place the cans in the same location somewhere sunny, such as a window ledge.

5. Measure the temperature of the water in each can after five, ten and 15 minutes.

6. Write the temperatures in the table each time.

7. Which can was the better reflector of heat radiation?

8. How do you know this?

9. Which can was the better absorber of heat radiation?

10. How do you know this?

Different surfaces do not emit and absorb heat radiation to the same extent.

- Surfaces that are matt (dull and dark) are the best absorbers and the best emitters.
- Surfaces that are light and shiny are the poorest absorbers and the poorest emitters.

Check your understanding

1. Fig 7.42 shows details of a solar panel that is used for heating water.

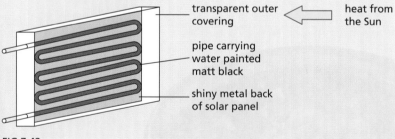

transparent outer covering ← heat from the Sun

pipe carrying water painted matt black

shiny metal back of solar panel

FIG 7.42

Explain each of the following features.

a) The panel has a transparent outer covering rather than a wooden outer covering.

b) The pipe is made of copper and not plastic.

c) The pipe is painted matt black.

d) The back of the panel is shiny metal.

C- PENTANE
C- PENTAN

FIG 7.43 The coil on the back of a refrigerator is painted matt black so that the maximum amount of heat radiation will be emitted. Heat is also lost from the coil by convection through the air

Key terms

emit give out

absorb take in

Thermal insulators and conductors

We are learning how to:

- distinguish between thermal insulators and conductors
- appreciate how thermal conductors and insulators are used.

Thermal insulators and conductors »

A **thermal insulator** is a material that is a poor conductor of heat. Thermal insulators include wood, plastics, ceramics and glass.

FIG 7.44 Pans often have handles made of wood or plastic so that they can be held while food is being cooked

FIG 7.45 Glass is such a poor conductor of heat that a glass blow can hold both ends of a glass tube while heating the middle

FIG 7.46 Food stays hot for a long time in a ceramic dish because ceramics are good thermal insulators

Activity 7.10

To compare how quickly heat travels through metal and plastic

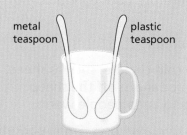

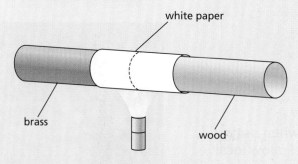

Here is what you need:

- plastic teaspoon
- metal teaspoon
- cup of hot water
- stopwatch.

SAFETY

Take care when heating. Follow local regulations.

Here is what you should do:

1. Start the stopwatch.

   metal teaspoon   plastic teaspoon

2. Place the teaspoons in the hot water at the same time and hold them there, one in each hand.

3. After two minutes, can you feel a difference in the temperature of the two spoons?

   FIG 7.47

Check your understanding

1. In an experiment, a strip of white paper was wound around a rod. One half of the rod was brass and the other half was wood.

   white paper

   brass

   wood

   FIG 7.48

   When the paper was passed over a flame several times the part wrapped around the wood was scorched but the part wrapped around the brass was not. Explain why.

Fun fact

Space shuttles used to be used to make regular trips between the Earth and space. When a space shuttle re-entered the Earth's atmosphere from space, the underside got extremely hot due to friction with the air.

FIG 7.49

The underside of the space shuttle was covered in ceramic tiles that protected the craft from this potentially damaging heat.

Key term

thermal insulator a material that is a poor conductor of heat

Air as a heat insulator

We are learning how to:

- distinguish between thermal insulators and conductors
- explain the importance of air as a thermal insulator.

Trapped air »»

Heat is conducted through materials as a result of movement energy being passed from one particle to the next. The particles in a gas are much further away from each other than in a solid or a liquid. Gases are therefore poor conductors of heat.

Trapped air can be used as an **insulator**.

Wool keeps animals that live in a cold climate, such as sheep, warm in the winter. The wool can be shorn off the sheep and used to knit woollen jumpers to keep people warm.

Fibreglass consists of many layers of glass fibres. Small pockets of air are trapped between the fibres giving this material excellent insulating properties.

Bird feathers are sometimes used to stuff duvets because of their insulating properties.

FIG 7.50 Wool is a natural fibre that is able to trap air

FIG 7.51 Fibreglass is often used to insulate the roof space of buildings to reduce heat loss

Activity 7.11

Which material is the best insulator?

Here is what you need:

- four beakers
- four thermometers
- four types of insulating material
- cardboard
- scissors
- hot water
- measuring cylinder.

⚠ **SAFETY**
Take care when using hot water. Follow local regulations.

Here is what you should do:

1. Cover the bottom and sides of four beakers, each with a different insulating material.

FIG 7.52 In cold weather, birds are able to fluff their feathers out to trap air between the feathers and reduce the loss of heat from the body

2. Cut out four cardboard lids for your beakers. Mark the lids A, B, C and D.

3. Make a small hole in the centre of each lid large enough to push a thermometer through.

4. Using a measuring cylinder, put an equal volume of hot water into each of the beakers.

5. Place the lids on the beakers and record the initial temperature of the hot water.

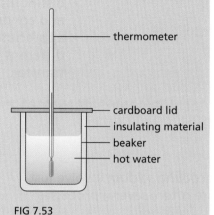

— thermometer
— cardboard lid
— insulating material
— beaker
— hot water

FIG 7.53

6. Measure the temperature of the water in each beaker every two minutes.

7. Record your values in a table.

8. Use your data to draw a graph of temperature against time for each insulating material on the same grid.

9. From your graphs, decide which material is the best insulator and which is the poorest.

Check your understanding

1. In some countries buildings have outer and inner walls. A building can be insulated by filling the cavity with plastic foam containing bubbles of air.

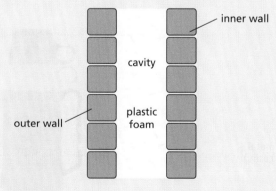

inner wall

cavity

outer wall

plastic foam

FIG 7.54

a) Explain how heat could be lost from the inner wall to the outer wall across the cavity.

b) Explain why filling the cavity with plastic reduces heat loss.

Key term

insulator material that reduces heat transfer

195

Total heat transfer

- distinguish between thermal insulators and conductors
- appreciate the contribution of different processes to total heat transfer.

Total heat transfer >>>

Everyday examples of heating or cooling seldom involve just one method of heat transfer. More often, several processes occur together.

A device that is designed to control the transfer of heat must take into account all three methods of heat transfer.

A vacuum flask is designed to keep liquids hot on a cold day or cold on a hot day. To do this, it must reduce heat transfer by conduction, convection and radiation.

The vacuum flask contains a glass vessel, which has an inner and outer wall. The air is removed from between the walls to leave a vacuum. The inner surfaces of the vessel are silvered. The flask is sealed by a cork stopper and plastic cap. The table on the next page shows how the features of the vacuum flask reduce heat transfer.

FIG 7.56 In a wood-burning stove heat is transferred through the metal stove by conduction, the air in the room is heated by convection and the fire also gives out heat radiation

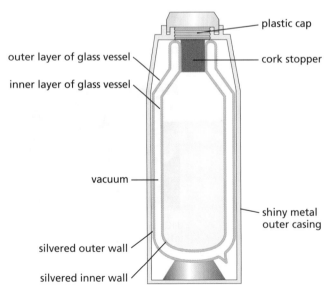

- plastic cap
- outer layer of glass vessel
- inner layer of glass vessel
- cork stopper
- vacuum
- shiny metal outer casing
- silvered outer wall
- silvered inner wall

FIG 7.57 Inside a vacuum flask

FIG 7.58 A vacuum flask keeps liquids hot on a cold day or cold on a hot day

Method of transfer	Feature of the vacuum flask
Conduction	The vessel is made of glass, which is a poor conductor. The stopper is made of cork and plastic, which are also poor conductors.
Convection	The vacuum between the inner and outer walls of the vessel prevents heat loss from the vessel by convection. Convection currents cannot form where there is no air.
Radiation	The inner surfaces of the vessel are silvered. The inner wall reflects heat radiation back into the vessel. This will prevent heat radiation leaving the flask so keeping the contents hot. The outer wall reflects heat radiation from outside the flask. This will prevent heat radiation entering the flask so keeping the contents cold.

TABLE 7.5

Activity 7.12

Examining a vacuum flask

Here is what you need:

- vacuum flask.

Here is what you should do:

1. Carefully examine the vacuum flask and identify the structures discussed in the lesson.

2. Note the different materials used to make the vacuum flask and consider whether they are thermal conductors or insulators.

3. Look at the mirrored surfaces and consider how reflecting heat radiation reduces the transfer of heat.

Fun fact

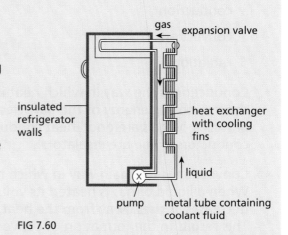

FIG 7.59 Cool bags are designed to reduce heat transfer by conduction and radiation

Check your understanding

1. Fig 7.60 is a diagram of a refrigerator.

   a) Explain why the refrigerator walls contains insulating material.

   b) Suggest a suitable material for insulating the refrigerator walls.

   c) Name the process by which heat is transferred:

      i) from the fluid through the metal tube

      ii) from the cooling fins into the room.

   d) Explain why the tube is made of metal and not plastic.

   e) Explain why there are fins on the heat exchanger.

   f) Explain why the cooling fins are painted matt black.

gas   expansion valve

insulated refrigerator walls

heat exchanger with cooling fins

liquid

pump   metal tube containing coolant fluid

FIG 7.60

197

Review of Thermal energy

- Heat is a form of energy and is measured in joules.

- The temperature of an object is a measure of the amount of heat energy it contains.

- When two objects of different temperature are placed together, heat energy passes from the hotter object to the cooler object until both objects are at the same temperature.

- Temperature is measured using a thermometer. The most common type of thermometer used in laboratories is called a liquid-in-glass thermometer. The liquid is usually alcohol (ethanol) (containing a dye to make it easier to see) or mercury.

- The top of a column of liquid is called the meniscus and it is not flat.
  - The meniscus of a thermometer containing alcohol dips down at the centre. The reading on an alcohol thermometer should be taken from the bottom of the meniscus.
  - The meniscus of a thermometer containing mercury rises up at the centre. The reading on a mercury thermometer should be taken from the top of the meniscus.

- Temperature is most often measured in degrees centigrade or Celsius. The symbol for this is °C.

- On the Celsius scale, pure water freezes at 0 °C and boils at 100 °C at normal atmospheric pressure.

- The kelvin scale is also sometimes used in science.
  - Value on Celsius scale = value on kelvin scale – 273
  - Value on kelvin scale = value on Celsius scale + 273

- Transfer of heat requires a difference of temperature.

- There are three different processes by which heat may be transferred:
  - conduction
  - convection
  - radiation.

- Conduction is the way in which heat is transferred through solids. Heat increases the movement energy of the particles in a solid and this is passed on to surrounding particles. Metals are good heat conductors while non-metals are generally poor heat conductors (some are insulators).

- Convection is the main way in which heat is transferred through liquids and gases. When a liquid or gas is heated its volume increases. As its volume increases its density decreases. It rises away from the heat source to be replaced by cooler liquid or gas. This results in the formation of convection currents.

- Radiation is the way in which heat is transferred across a vacuum. Heat radiation is sometimes called infrared radiation.

- Materials that are poor conductors of heat energy are called thermal insulators or just insulators.

- Air and other gases are poor conductors of heat. Many materials used as insulators, such as fibreglass, rock wool and expanded polystyrene, have pockets of gas trapped inside them.

- In real situations, heat transfer is seldom limited to just conduction, convection or radiation. Heat transfer is more often a combination of two or even all three of these processes.

- Devices used to prevent the passage of heat energy, such as the vacuum flask, must be designed to reduce conduction, convection and radiation.

Review questions on Thermal energy

1. Fig 7.RQ.1 shows a thermometer.

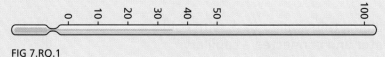

FIG 7.RQ.1

a) Copy Fig 7.RQ.1 and use a ruler to complete the scale between 0 and 100 °C.

b) Cyclohexane is a chemical that melts at 7 °C and boils at 81 °C. Mark these temperatures on your thermometer using 'M' for melts and 'B' for boils.

c) In what state is cyclohexane at room temperature?

d) Apart from being a liquid, state two other properties of mercury that make it suitable for use in a thermometer.

2. A student was asked to heat a beaker of water and record the temperature every minute for ten minutes. He placed the thermometer in the position shown in Fig 7.RQ.2.

a) Explain why the temperature shown on the thermometer is not likely to be the average temperature of the water in the beaker.

b) What should the student do to obtain a more accurate value for the temperature of the water in the beaker?

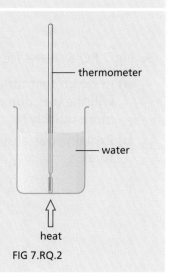

thermometer

water

heat

FIG 7.RQ.2

c) Fig 7.RQ.3 shows the temperature at the start and the end of heating.

FIG 7.RQ.3

i) What were the temperatures at the start and the end of heating?

ii) By how much had the temperature of the water increased?

d) Predict what would happen to the temperature rise if, during the same time period:

i) more heat energy was given to the same volume of water

ii) the same amount of heat energy was given to a larger volume of water.

3. Fig 7.RQ.4 shows a frying pan. It is composed of two materials, X and Y.

a) i) Suggest what material X could be.

ii) Explain your answer.

b) i) Suggest what material Y could be.

ii) Explain your answer.

FIG 7.RQ.4

4. A student filled a thin-walled flask with cold coloured water and connected a capillary tube to it.

She then held the flask in her hands for ten minutes.

a) What change was there to the apparatus?

b) Explain this change.

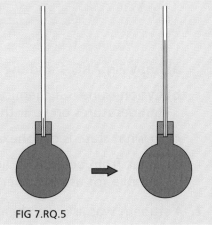

FIG 7.RQ.5

5. Fig 7.RQ.6 shows ice cubes being heated in test tubes A and B.

a) In which test tube will the ice cube melt more quickly?

b) Explain your answer to a).

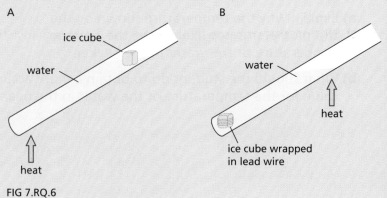

FIG 7.RQ.6

6. An electric heater was placed exactly between two cans holding equal volumes of water. The cans were identical except that one can was shiny silver (can A) and the other had been painted matt black (can B).

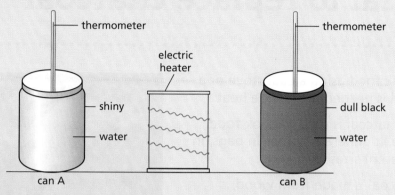

FIG 7.RQ.7

The temperature of the water in each can was measured every minute for a quarter of an hour. The data collected is given in the table.

Time (minutes)	Temperature of water in can A (°C)	Temperature of water in can B (°C)	Time (minutes)	Temperature of water in can A (°C)	Temperature of water in can B (°C)
0	20.0	20.0	8	24.0	25.5
1	20.5	20.5	9	25.0	26.5
2	20.5	21.0	10	25.5	28.0
3	21.0	21.5	11	26.5	29.0
4	21.5	22.5	12	27.5	30.5
5	22.0	23.0	13	28.5	31.5
6	23.0	24.0	14	29.5	33.0
7	23.5	25.0	15	31.0	34.5

TABLE 7.6

a) State three things that were kept the same to ensure that a fair comparison was made between the cans in this activity.

b) Name the main process by which heat energy is transferred from the electric heater to the two cans.

c) Plot graphs of temperature, on the y-axis, against time, on the x-axis, for can A and can B on the same grid.

d) Explain any difference in the graphs for the two cans.

Using a fuel made from recycled material to replace charcoal

In order to cook food using a coal stove or a jerk pan, a fuel is needed to provide heat.

Traditionally, charcoal is used to cook food on a coal stove. It generally comes in bags, in chunks of different sizes.

Although charcoal is made from wood, which is a renewable source of energy, its manufacture damages the environment and creates pollution.

Every year as a society, we produce millions of tonnes of waste paper and cardboard. Much of this can be recycled.

FIG 7.SIP.1 Charcoal provides the heat to barbeque food

1. You are going to work in a group of three or four to manufacture briquettes from waste paper and cardboard. The tasks are:

   - to research about charcoal that is currently for sale in your community
   - to identify sources of waste paper and/or cardboard that you think might make a good fuel
   - to devise a method of manufacturing briquettes from waste paper/cardboard
   - to compare how well your briquettes burn compared to commercially available charcoal
   - to compile a report accompanied by a slideshow presentation which includes photographs and/or a video sequence showing how you made your briquettes and how well they burn.

FIG 7.SIP.2 Making charcoal is harmful to the environment

a) Take a look at the different brands of charcoal for sale in your local market or supermarket. Measure the sizes of the chunks. This will give you some idea what size to make your briquettes. Ask the shop assistant which brand is the most

FIG 7.SIP.3 Paper and cardboard waste

popular. Why does he or she think this is the case? What are the important features of the most popular brand?

b) Identify sources of waste paper and/or cardboard that can be used to make briquettes. Carry out some preliminary experiments to see if some types of paper and cardboard burn more easily than others. For example, is it easier to light a page of a newspaper or a page from a glossy magazine?

Are there any other issues to be taken into consideration? For example, your briquettes are going to heat food; do some types of paper or cardboard emit noxious fumes that would spoil the food?

c) Make some briquettes.

FIG 7.SIP.4 Hand-made briquettes dried by the sun

A simple way to make briquettes is to soak strips of paper in water and then shape them into 'logs' with your hands. Squeeze as much water as you can out of them and leave them to dry in the sun. When the logs have dried out they can be used as fuel.

Can you modify this method to make briquettes?

d) Devise a way to compare how well your briquettes burn with the commercially available charcoal.

For example, you could investigate how easy it is to start your briquettes burning compared to charcoal. Once burning, you could record how long the two fuels burn. You might make observations such as how much smoke each fuel produces and how much is left after burning.

e) You should record such things as:

- the composition of your briquettes
- your method of making briquettes
- whether your fuel stayed alight and glowed like charcoal
- whether your fuel burnt as long as charcoal.

You should take some photographs or video sequences when testing your briquettes.

Use the information you have gathered to prepare an illustrated slideshow presentation. You should be prepared to explain why you chose a particular way to make briquettes and to discuss how they performed. You should also discuss possible changes to your method as a result of the experience you have gained thus far.

Unit 8: Energy in ecosystems

The importance of sunlight ≫

The Sun provides all of the energy needed to maintain life. Green plants capture this energy.

FIG 8.1 Green plants capture energy from the Sun

Without the Sun's energy life would not exist on Earth.

Feeding

Some animals, such as sheep and goats, feed directly on plants.

FIG 8.2 Sheep and goats eat leaves and grass

Some animals eat other animals.

FIG 8.3 Sheath-tailed bats feed on insects that they catch in flight

Some animals eat both plants and other animals.

FIG 8.4 Tayras eat fruit as well as other small animals

Interdependence

Plant and animal species do not live in isolation in an ecosystem but rely on each other for food and the nutrients and energy they obtain from it.

Challenge

FIG 8.5 Krill are tiny animals that live in huge numbers in the world's oceans

How do you think the numbers of big fish would be affected by a fall in the numbers of krill? Why do you think this?

What is an ecosystem?

We are learning how to:

- illustrate energy flow from the Sun to plants and animals
- appreciate what an ecosystem is.

Ecosystems >>>

Ecology is the study of how organisms interact with each other and how they interact with the physical and chemical factors of their environment.

An **ecosystem** is a unit of the natural world. Each ecosystem can be conveniently divided into **biotic** and **abiotic** factors.

FIG 8.6 **a)** Biotic (living) factors **b)** Abiotic (non-living things)

Biotic factors are those that relate to living things. These are the plants and animals that live in an ecosystem. Abiotic factors are those that relate to non-living things such as rock outcrops and the shape of the ground. Conditions like temperature and humidity are also abiotic factors. Biotic and abiotic factors interact to provide a stable self-sustaining system.

A **habitat** is the place where an organism lives. For example, a habitat might be a pond, a rock pool or a desert. Within an ecosystem there may be a number of different habitats that are linked together.

FIG 8.7 Examples of ecosystems: **a)** Sea shore **b)** Riverbank **c)** Coral reef **d)** Desert

Activity 8.1

Identifying different local habitats

Here is what you need:

- notebook
- digital camera if available.

 SAFETY

Follow local regulations when carrying out fieldwork. Wash your hands at the end of the activity. Do not touch any plants or animals.

Here is what you should do:

1. Visit some local habitats such as the school garden, a pond, a river, a wood and so on.

2. Make notes on the main features of each habitat.

3. Take photographs of each habitat.

4. Use your notes and pictures to write a brief description of each habitat.

5. State ways in which habitats are similar and ways in which they are different.

An **ecological niche** is the role that an organism has in a habitat. Organisms may occupy the same habitat but have different niches. For example, both caterpillars and aphids are found living on plants but the caterpillars eat leaves while the aphids feed on sap.

The **population** of a species is the number of that species living in a habitat. Populations change over time. A **community** is the collective term for all of the populations of organisms that live together in a habitat.

Check your understanding

1. Populations of different organisms live in a pond.

   a) What is the collective term for populations in a habitat?

   b) Give two examples of the following in the pond:

   i) biotic factors

   ii) abiotic factors.

   c) Suggest one way in which the populations of organisms in a pond interact with each other.

Fun fact

Organisms that live in a desert have found ways to survive the harsh climate. For example, plants conserve water and animals only come out at night when it is cooler.

Key terms

ecology the study of how organisms interact with each other and their environment

ecosystem a unit of the natural world

biotic relates to living things

abiotic non-living features of an environment

habitat place where an organism lives

ecological niche role that an organism has in a habitat

population number of a species living in a habitat

community the collective term for all of the populations of organisms that live together in a habitat

Creating an ecosystem

We are learning how to:

- illustrate energy flow from the Sun to plants and animals
- create an ecosystem.

Creating an ecosystem »

Before you start to design your ecosystem, you need to decide what habitats you would like and what organisms they will attract. Here are some examples.

FIG 8.8 A small, well-designed, school garden can have several different habitats that will each attract populations of different animals and plants

FIG 8.9 Flowers will attract butterflies, bees and other insects, as well as the birds that feed on them, and make your garden attractive

FIG 8.10 Berries are a good food source and will attract birds and small mammals like mice

FIG 8.11 Rotting wood releases nutrients back into the soil but it also provides an ideal habitat for animals like beetles and woodlice. Different types of fungi and mosses will grow on the wood

FIG 8.12 A small pond provides a habitat for fish and insects, as well as a place for amphibians like frogs to breed

Lots of animals will be attracted to the water to drink.

Activity 8.2

Creating a school garden

This is a whole-class activity that will be coordinated by the teacher.

Here is what you need:

- notebook
- tape measure
- pegs
- gardening tools
- shrubs and plants
- pond liner.

 SAFETY
Take care when carrying out practical activities. Wash your hands at the end of the activity. Wear protective gloves when handling plants. Follow local safety regulations.

Here is what you should do:

1. Draw a plan of the piece of ground that is going to become the school garden.

2. Decide on what habitats you would like to create.

3. On your plan, mark in those habitats and where they will be.

4. Plan how to create each habitat separately. One group could take on responsibility for each habitat. Use the internet and books to help you.

5. Gather the materials and tools you will need.

6. Create your habitat.

Check your understanding

1. A school garden could include small fruit trees.

   Suggest three ways in which animals might benefit from such trees.

Photosynthesis

We are learning how to:

- illustrate energy flow from the Sun to plants and animals
- appreciate the importance of photosynthesis to all living things.

Using the Sun's energy

The source of energy for any ecosystem is the Sun. This provides the energy needed for the process of **photosynthesis**, without which there would be no plants or animals.

Plant leaves are green because the cells contain a pigment called **chlorophyll**. This pigment is able to trap the sunlight that falls on the leaf and use it to bring about the following chemical reaction:

carbon dioxide + water ⟶ glucose + oxygen

The plant absorbs carbon dioxide from the atmosphere through the leaves, and water from the ground through the roots.

Oxygen is released to the atmosphere and the glucose is stored in the leaf as starch until it is needed by the plant.

FIG 8.13 Photosynthesis is the process by which green plants make their own food

Activity 8.3

To show that sunlight is necessary for photosynthesis

Here is what you need:

- green plant
- dark cupboard
- card
- scissors
- two paperclips
- materials for starch test.

 SAFETY

Take care when handling plants. Follow local safety regulations when carrying out practical work. Wash your hands at the end of the activity.

Here is what you should do:

1. Place a green plant in a dark cupboard for one week and water it each day. This will remove any starch stored in the leaves.

2. Cut out two pieces of card about the same size as one of the plant leaves.

3. Cut a hole in the centre of one of the pieces of card. This can be any shape you choose.

4. Using a paperclip, place the two pieces of card either side of a leaf. The piece that has the hole should be on the upper surface of the leaf, which will receive most of the sunlight.

5. Place the plant in a sunny position for one day.

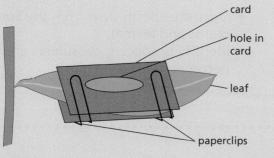

FIG 8.14

6. Remove the leaf from between the cards and test it for starch using iodine solution. If starch is present in any part of the leaf, it will turn blue-black.

7. Which part of the leaf gave a positive test and which gave a negative test?

FIG 8.15 Variegated leaves

Some plants have leaves that are not completely green and have areas that appear light yellow or white. There are areas of the leaf that do not contain the green pigment chlorophyll. These are called variegated leaves.

Variegated leaves can be used to show that chlorophyll is necessary for photosynthesis.

When a variegated leaf is tested for the presence of starch, only those parts that are green will turn blue-black. No starch is present in those parts of the leaf that do not have chlorophyll.

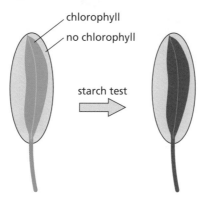

FIG 8.16 Starch test on a variegated leaf

> **Fun fact**
>
> The leaves of all green plants contain chlorophyll.
>
>
>
> FIG 8.18 Sometimes chlorophyll is masked by other pigments

Check your understanding

1. Fig 8.17 shows a plant growing under a bell jar. The dish contains a substance called soda lime, which absorbs carbon dioxide from the air.

How could you use this plant and apparatus to demonstrate that photosynthesis requires carbon dioxide?

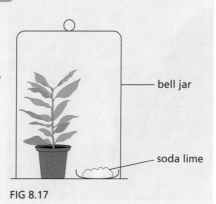

FIG 8.17

Key terms

photosynthesis the process by which green plants make their own food

chlorophyll the green pigment in leaves

Producers, consumers and decomposers

We are learning how to:

- illustrate energy flow from the Sun to plants and animals
- identify producers, consumers and decomposers.

Producers and consumers ⟫

Organisms may be placed into groups according to whether they produce or consume food.

FIG 8.19 Green plants are called **producers** because they use energy from sunlight to produce the food

Green plants use some of the food themselves and what remains is often eaten by animals.

FIG 8.20 Animals are called **consumers** because they consume the food made by green plants

Key terms

producers plants that use energy from sunlight to produce the food

consumers living things that consume the food made by green plants

herbivores animals that eat only plants

primary consumers consume food from green plants directly

carnivores animals that eat only other animals

secondary consumers eat the animals that eat only plants

decomposers feed on dead organic material

Animals that eat only plants are called **herbivores**. Herbivores such as cattle are **primary consumers** because they eat plants directly.

Animals that eat only other animals are called **carnivores**. Carnivores like the leopard are **secondary consumers**. They do not eat plants directly but eat herbivores that themselves eat plants.

Decomposers

There is another important group of organisms, which feed on dead organic material. This might be dead plants and animals or animal waste. This group is called the **decomposers**.

Some decomposers, such as bacteria, are so small that they can only be seen with the help of a microscope. Fungi are decomposers. They often grow on decaying plant material or on animal waste.

FIG 8.21 Carnivores such as leopards are secondary consumers

Although decomposing organic material does not look or smell very nice, decomposers do an extremely important job. By breaking down the waste, nutrients are released into the soil that can be used again by other organisms.

Activity 8.4

Identifying producers, consumers and decomposers

Your teacher will lead this activity.

Here is what you need:

- notebook.

Here is what you should do:

1. Take a short walk around the school compound or the grounds nearby.

2. Make a note of any organisms you see and decide if they are producers, consumers or decomposers.

3. Make lists of the three groups of organisms.

Check your understanding

1. Maize grows in a field. The maize plants are eaten by locusts. The locusts are eaten by lizards.

    a) State whether each of the organisms described is a primary consumer, a secondary consumer or a producer.

    b) How are the nutrients contained in the bodies of these animals ultimately returned to the ground?

FIG 8.22 Worms are decomposers: as they feed, they move organic waste through the soil

Fun fact

Vultures are scavengers.

FIG 8.23 Scavengers are secondary consumers that do not kill primary consumers but feed on their dead bodies

Food chains

We are learning how to:

- illustrate energy flow from the Sun to plants and animals
- draw and interpret a food chain.

Food chains

Organisms can be grouped as producers or consumers depending on whether they make food or eat food. The relationship between the two groups can be shown as:

producers ⟶ consumers

The arrow joining the two groups of organisms can be interpreted in several ways.

- It can be taken to mean 'is eaten by' – producers are eaten by consumers.

- It shows the transfer of energy – consumers obtain energy by eating producers.

- It shows the transfer of nutrients – consumers obtain nutrients by eating producers.

If you show this relationship using the names of organisms, the result is called a **food chain**.

Grass ⟶ Rabbit

You can add to this food chain.

Grass ⟶ Rabbit ⟶ Ocelot

At each link in the food chain, energy and nutrients pass from one organism to the next.

Plant ⟶ Insect ⟶ Lizard ⟶ Snake ⟶ Hawk

There are two important facts that are true of all food chains.

1. A food chain always starts with a producer – a green plant or something formed from it.

2. All of the energy that passes along a food chain comes from the Sun.

FIG 8.24 A rabbit is a herbivore and therefore a primary consumer

FIG 8.25 A rabbit may be eaten by a carnivore (secondary consumer) such as an ocelot

Making food chains using name cards and arrow cards

Here is what you need:

- 12 blank cards (4 cm × 3 cm).

Here is what you should do:

1. Make name cards for each of these organisms: plant, insect, worm, picoplat, rabbit, keskidee, mouse, snake, hawk.

2. Make three arrow cards.

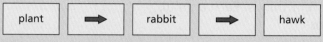

FIG 8.26 An example of a food chain

3. Use your cards to make some food chains. Each of your food chains:

- should start with a plant
- should have at least three organisms.

4. Write down your food chains.

> **Fun fact**
>
> The numbers of organisms in each population decreases along a food chain. In the food chain described there are many grass plants, a small number of rabbits and an even smaller number of ocelots.

Key term

food chain relationship between producers and consumers using the names of organisms

The general flow diagram for a food chain is:

Producer $\longrightarrow$ Primary consumer $\longrightarrow$ Secondary consumer

A food chain may have more than one secondary consumer.

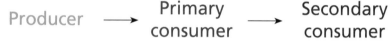

Grass $\longrightarrow$ Grasshopper $\longrightarrow$ Rat $\longrightarrow$ Snake $\longrightarrow$ Falcon

Check your understanding

1. Fig 8.27 shows a food chain from a lake in Europe.

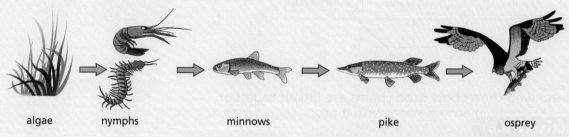

algae   nymphs   minnows   pike   osprey

FIG 8.27

a) Which organism feeds on

i) algae?

ii) nymphs?

iii) minnows?

iv) pike?

b) From the organisms in the food chain, name:

i) a primary consumer

ii) a secondary consumer

iii) a producer.

Food webs

We are learning how to:

- illustrate energy flow from the Sun to plants and animals
- draw and interpret a food web.

Food webs »»

A food chain shows each animal eating one other type of organism. In the real world, animals eat lots of different things. Each animal, therefore, will appear in many food chains.

Here are some food chains involving organisms that live in a desert.

Desert plants ⟶ Insects ⟶ Large lizards ⟶ Hawks

Desert plants ⟶ Small lizards ⟶ Large lizards ⟶ Hawks

Desert plants ⟶ Kangaroo rats ⟶ Snakes ⟶ Hawks

Desert plants ⟶ Small lizards ⟶ Snakes ⟶ Hawks

Most of the organisms are in more than one food chain. The feeding relationships between these organisms are better shown as a **food web**.

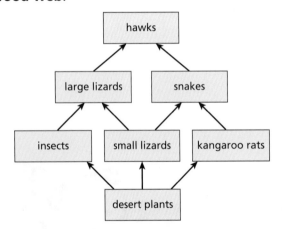

FIG 8.28 Food web

A food web shows how food chains are linked together.

Activity 8.6

Observing feeding relationships

Here is what you need:

- notebook
- hand lens.

 SAFETY

Follow local regulations when carrying out practical work. Wash your hands after the activity. Do not touch plants or animals.

Here is what you should do:

1. Go out into the area around the school and observe what different animals feed on. For example, on what flowers do insects feed? On what insects do small animals feed? On what small animals do large animals feed?
2. Construct one or more food chains using your observations.
3. If possible, use your food chains to construct a food web.

The organisms in a food web can be organised into a **trophic pyramid**, where organisms occupy different **trophic levels**.

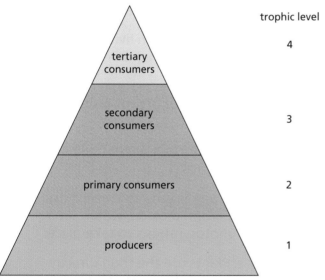

FIG 8.29 The width of the trophic pyramid indicates the numbers of organisms, the total mass of the organisms or the amount of energy available at each level

Each level of the pyramid is occupied by a different organism. At the top of the pyramid are tertiary consumers such as hawks, which eat secondary consumers. Can you explain why a hawk needs a large area in which to hunt if it is to obtain sufficient food?

Check your understanding

1. Here are some feeding relationships between animals in a woodland.

   - Worms, voles and mice eat vegetation.
   - Badgers eat worms, voles and mice.
   - Shrews and badgers eat worms.
   - Barn owls eat shrews, voles and mice.

   Show this information as a food web.

Fun fact

Food webs for a large ecosystem might contain many organisms.

Key terms

food web shows relationships between animals that are in more than one food chain

trophic pyramid diagram showing relative number of organisms at each level of a food web

trophic level a level in the trophic pyramid

Review of Energy in ecosystems

- Ecology is the study of how organisms interact with each other and the environment.

- An ecosystem is a unit of the natural world. It has both biotic and abiotic factors.
  - Biotic factors are concerned with living things and relate to the organisms that live within an ecosystem.
  - Abiotic factors are concerned with non-living things and include factors such as temperature, humidity, purity of air and so on.

- Within any ecosystem there might be a number of habitats. A habitat is a place where organisms live. Examples of habitats include a pond, a rock pool, a forest and a desert.

- An ecological niche is the role that an organism has in a habitat. A number of organisms may occupy the same habitat but have different niches.

- The population of a species within a habitat is the number of them living there at that particular time. The sizes of populations change over time for a number of different reasons.

- A community is the collective term for all of the populations of organisms that live together in a habitat.

- Even a small ecosystem may have several different habitats. Each habitat will attract different organisms.

- Photosynthesis is the process in which energy from the Sun is used to convert carbon dioxide and water into food, in the form of glucose. Carbon dioxide, water, sunlight and the green pigment chlorophyll are essential for photosynthesis to take place.

- All life on the Earth is dependent on photosynthesis. Plants use the food directly. Animals either eat the plants (herbivores) or eat the animals that eat plants (carnivores).

- Green plants are called producers because they use energy from sunlight to produce the food.

- Animals are called consumers because they consume the food made by green plants.
  - Primary consumers eat the plants directly.
  - Secondary consumers eat the animals that eat plants.

- Decomposers break down organic material, releasing nutrients back into the ecosystem for use again by living organisms.

- The relationship between producers and consumers can be shown as:

Producers ⟶ Consumers

When the names of organisms are included the result is called a food chain.

- The arrow joining groups of organisms in a food chain can be interpreted as:
  - 'is eaten by'
  - transfer of energy
  - transfer of nutrients.
- All food chains:
  - start with a producer
  - are driven by energy from the Sun.
- A food web shows the feeding relationship between a number of different organisms and is a combination of a number of food chains.
- The organisms in a food web occupy different trophic levels. The number of organisms in the population decreases as you rise up these levels.

Review questions for Energy in ecosystems

1. Here are the names of some habitats.

pond　　　　**seashore**　　　　**soil**　　　　**trees**

Match each of the following organisms to one of these habitats:

a) crab　　　　　　　　　　**b)** worm

c) keskidee　　　　　　　　**d)** frog.

2. Fig 8.RQ.1 shows a food chain.

weeds　　　　tadpoles　　　　minnows　　　　perch

FIG 8.RQ.1

a) In which habitat do these organisms live?

b) Which organism is the primary consumer?

c) Which two animals in the food chain are carnivores?

d) State three ways in which the arrows in the food chain can be interpreted.

3. Explain the meaning of the following terms:

a) producer

b) community

c) secondary consumer

d) ecological niche.

4. a) Write a word equation for photosynthesis, including any necessary conditions for the process to take place.

b) The plant in Fig 8.RQ.2 is unusual in that part of the stem and some of the leaves are white.

To obtain new plants, two cuttings, X and Y, were taken. They were treated in exactly the same way. Cutting Y flourished while cutting X died. Explain why.

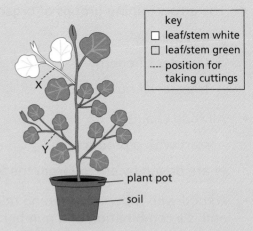

FIG 8.RQ.2

5. Fig 8.RQ.3 shows part of a food web for a pond.

a) What is the source of the energy that drives this food web?

b) Name a secondary consumer in the food web.

c) From this food web, write a food chain that contains at least three organisms.

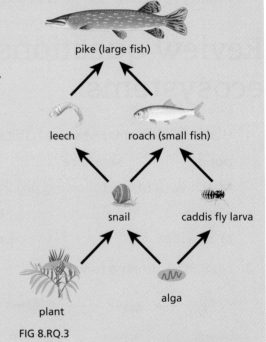

FIG 8.RQ.3

6. Fig 8.RQ.4 shows a habitat along a sea shore.

a) Suggest a descriptive name for this habitat.

b) Name three populations of organisms that you might expect to find in this habitat.

c) How can several different populations of organisms flourish in the same habitat?

FIG 8.RQ.4

7. Fig 8.RQ.5 shows a food web for a rocky shore.

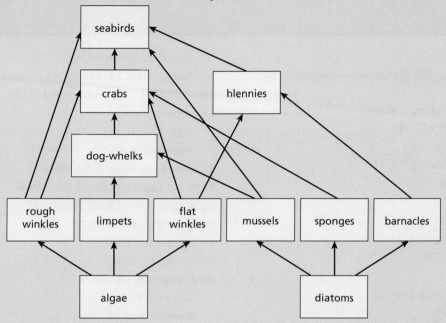

FIG 8.RQ.5

a) What is passed on from one organism to the next in each step of a food web?

b) What name is given to the organisms in the lowest trophic level of a food chain?

c) How many primary consumers are shown in the food web?

d) Write down the two longest food chains in this food web.

8. The following shows the positions of decomposers in a food chain.

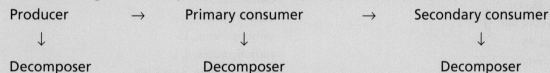

a) Why are decomposers linked to each member of the food chain?

b) Name two organisms that are decomposers.

c) Explain the importance of decomposers.

Index

population, of species, 207
primary consumers, 212, 213
principle of moments, 154–155
    proving, 156–157
producers, 212–213
product, of chemical reactions, 91
proteases, 16, 17
proteins, 8, 9, 23
    food test for, 22, 22*f*
pulse rate, 39, 48–49, 48*f*
    of adult, 49
    exercise and, 50–51

Q
qualitative physical properties, 83
quantitative physical properties, 83

R
radial pulse, 48, 48*f*
radiation, 180, 181, 188–191
    emitting and absorbing, 190–191
reactants, 91
recrystallise, 103
recycled material, fuel from, 202–203
red blood cells, 46, 47, 47*t*
residue, 115
respiration, cell, 60, 68–69, 68*f*
respiratory system
    parts of, 62. *see also* specific parts
    structure of, 60, 62–63, 62*f*
reversible change, 87
rusting, 94, 95

S
saliva, 15
salt, 93
saturated solutions, 100–101
secondary consumers, 212, 213
second-order levers, 158, 158*f*
sediment, 127
sedimentation, 127, 127*f*
seesaw, 154, 154*f*, 155
separating funnel, 124, 124*f*, 125
separation, mixtures, 112–113
    centrifugation, 126–127, 126*f*
    distillation. *see* distillation
    evaporation, 116, 117

physical, 114–115
    sedimentation, 127, 127*f*
septum, 42, 43
Shepard, Alan, 147
sieving, 115
simple sugars, 20, 21
small intestine, 16, 17
smoking, 61
    and cancer, 74, 74*f*
    and circulation problem, 74–75
    and emphysema, 75, 75*f*
snakes, 19
solid–liquid mixture, 112
solubilities, 123
soluble, 97
solute, crystals, 97
solutions, 96–97
    concentration, 98–99
    dilute, 98, 99
    saturated, 100–101
    supersaturated, 102–103, 102*f*
solvent, 123
space shuttles, 193
speed, 132, 134–135
    calculation of, 136–137
speedometers, 135
sphygmomanometer, 52, 53
stability, 133
    equilibrium and, 166–167
stable, 164
stable equilibrium, 167*f*
starch, 20, 21
stomach, 16, 16*f*, 17
stroke, 32, 33
sumo wrestlers, 29
sunlight, importance of, 204
supersaturated solutions, 102–103, 102*f*
suspension, 105
systole, 42–43
systolic pressure, 52, 53

T
teeth, 14–15, 14*f*
temperature, 172
    heat and, 174–175
    measurement, 176–177
thermal energy, 172–173, 174, 175 *see also* heat

Acknowledgements

pp6-7: Anastasiia Malinich, pp6: Burke/Triolo Productions/Getty Images, pp6: Robert Manella/Getty Images, pp7: Holbox/Shutterstock, pp8: Elena Elisseeva/Shutterstock, pp8: Bonchan/Shutterstock, pp8: Matthew Bechelli/Shutterstock, pp9: Fotofreaks/Shutterstock, pp10: Elena Schweitzer/Shutterstock, pp12: Jake Lyell/Alamy, pp12: Dallas Stribley/Getty Images, pp12: Photofusion/Getty Images, pp12: Blacqbook/iStockphoto/Getty Images, pp12: Avava/Shutterstock, pp19: Sugar0607/iStockphoto, pp19: Gayvoronskaya Yana/Shutterstock, pp19: Eric Isselee/Shutterstock, pp20: ANDREW LAMBERT PHOTOGRAPHY/SCIENCE PHOTO LIBRARY, pp20: Martyn F. Chillmaid/Science Source, pp21: SATURN STILLS/SCIENCE PHOTO LIBRARY, pp27: Daniel Adongo/Getty Images, pp28: Bob Krist/Corbis, pp28: Florian Kopp / imageBROKER/Rex Features, pp28: Cassiede alain/Shutterstock, pp29: Peter Brooker/Rex Features, pp29: Rohit Seth/Shutterstock, pp30: ImageBROKER/Alamy Stock Photo, pp30: Helene Rogers/Art Directors & TRIP/Alamy Stock Photo, pp30: Anthony Strack/Gallo Images/Getty Images, pp30: Kurhan/Shutterstock, pp30: Michaeljung/Shutterstock, pp30: Sergey Novikov/Shutterstock, pp32: Digitalskille/Getty Images, pp33: Cultura/Rex Features, pp38: www.royaltystockphoto.com/Shutterstock, pp39: Science Photo Library/Ian Hooton / Science Source/Science Photo Library, pp39: Michaeljung/Shutterstock, pp47: Steve Debenport/Getty Images, pp49: Joel Shawn/Shutterstock, pp50: John Cole/Science Photo Library, pp51: Erik van Hannen/Getty Images, pp51: Wavebreakmedia/Shutterstock, pp53: Roblan/Shutterstock, pp54: Jubal Harshaw/Shutterstock, pp58: Jeffrey Blackler/Alamy Stock Photo, pp58: robertharding/Alamy Stock Photo, pp60: Anthony Asael/Art in All of Us/Corbis, pp60: Tewan Banditrukkanka/Shutterstock, pp60: Randimal/Shutterstock, pp63: Aaron Huey/National Geographic Creative/Corbis, pp65: Fiona Bailey/Stockim/Alamy, pp65: Ugo Montaldo/Shutterstock, pp67: Yon Marsh/Alamy, pp69: MICROSCAPE/Science Photo Library, pp69: Jose Luis Calvo/Shutterstock, pp70: Bog Dan/Anadolu Agency/Getty Images, pp70: MickyWiswedel/Shutterstock, pp72: Reynold Mainse/Design Pics/Corbis, pp72: Lucian Coman/Shutterstock, pp74: Vetpathologist/Shutterstock, pp75: Andrey Popov/Shutterstock, pp78: Mooredesigns/Shutterstock, pp80: Claffra/Shutterstock, pp80: You can more/Shutterstock, pp80: Erasmus Wolff/Shutterstock, pp81: Lighttraveler/Shutterstock, pp88: Michael Krinke/iStockphoto, pp88: MARTYN F. CHILLMAID/SCIENCE PHOTO LIBRARY, pp88: Pavel Vakhrushev/Shutterstock, pp90: ANDREW LAMBERT PHOTOGRAPHY/SCIENCE PHOTO LIBRARY, pp90: CHARLES D. WINTERS/SCIENCE PHOTO LIBRARY, pp90: ANDREW LAMBERT PHOTOGRAPHY/SCIENCE PHOTO LIBRARY, pp91: Science Photo Library, pp94: Pattara puttiwong/Shutterstock, pp94: Geo-grafika/Shutterstock, pp94: Foxtography/Shutterstock, pp95: TREVOR CLIFFORD PHOTOGRAPHY/SCIENCE PHOTO LIBRARY, pp95: Pyty/Shutterstock, pp96: TREVOR CLIFFORD PHOTOGRAPHY/SCIENCE PHOTO LIBRARY, pp97: MARTYN F. CHILLMAID/SCIENCE PHOTO LIBRARY, pp103: Charles D Winters/Getty Images, pp103: Science Photo Library, pp103: Creative Family/Shutterstock, pp105: Trish Gant/Getty Images, pp105: MARTYN F. CHILLMAID/Science Photo Library, pp105: Severija/Shutterstock, pp105: Urbanbuzz/Shutterstock, pp106: Prill/Shutterstock, pp106: Africa Studio/Shutterstock, pp107: Tero Hakala/Shutterstock, pp107: Vladimir Melnikov/Shutterstock, pp107: Phloen/Shutterstock, pp112: Louise murray/Alamy, pp112: GEOFF TOMPKINSON/SCIENCE PHOTO LIBRARY, pp113: PAUL RAPSON/SCIENCE PHOTO LIBRARY, pp113: CHARLES D. WINTERS/SCIENCE PHOTO LIBRARY, pp119: David Lefranc/Corbis, pp123: ANDREW LAMBERT PHOTOGRAPHY/SCIENCE PHOTO LIBRARY, pp124: Marko Bradic/Shutterstock, pp126: KLAUS GULDBRANDSEN/Science Photo Library, pp126: Praisaeng/Shutterstock, pp127: lyzs/Westend61/Corbis, pp130: Lebedinski Vladislav/Shutterstock, pp130: Sukpaiboonwat/Shutterstock, pp130: Mykola N/Shutterstock, pp130: Mykola N/Shutterstock, pp131: Luisa Puccini/Shutterstock, pp132: Kim Karpeles/Alamy, pp132: Igor Karasi/Shutterstock, pp132: Mikhail Bakunovich/Shutterstock, pp133: Christopher Morris/Corbis, pp133: Melica/Shutterstock, pp134: Pete Saloutos/Getty Images, pp134: Jose Luis Pelaez Inc/Getty Images, pp135: Winai Tepsuttinun/Shutterstock, pp136: David J. Green/Alamy, pp136: Al Tielemans /Sports Illustrated/Getty Images, pp137: FABRICE COFFRINI/AFP/Getty Images, pp141: Ro-Ma Stock Photography/Getty Images, pp141: MARK GARLICK/SCIENCE PHOTO LIBRARY, pp143: Leo Mason/Leo Mason/Corbis, pp144: AAMIR QURESHI/AFP/Getty Images, pp144: Ejla/iStockphoto, pp144: luoman/iStockphoto, pp145: RFJ Photo/Shutterstock, pp146: Steve Hathaway/Getty Images, pp146: Aspen Photo/Shutterstock, pp147: Caspar Benson/fstop/Corbis, pp149: Bob Thomas/Getty Images, pp149: Cameron Spencer/Getty Images, pp150: Goran cakmazovic/Shutterstock, pp151: JOSE ANTONIO PEÑAS/SCIENCE PHOTO LIBRARY, pp152: Spiderstock/iStockphoto, pp153: Dave Porter Peterborough Uk/Getty Images, pp154: John Birdsall/Rex Features, pp155: REUTERS, pp158: Ray Evans/Alamy, pp159: Huronphoto/iStockphoto, pp162: Javi indy/Shutterstock, pp164: Duomo/CORBIS, pp164: Desmond Boylan/REUTERS, pp165: Design56/Shutterstock, pp165: Boris Stroujko/Shutterstock, pp167: Richard R Hansen/Getty Images, pp170: Nayoka/Shutterstock, pp170: Designsstock/Shutterstock, pp170: Enlightened Media/Shutterstock, pp172: Ron Sanford/Getty Images, pp172: art-pho/Shutterstock, pp172: Wavebreakmedia/Shutterstock, pp172: Maria Uspenskaya/Shutterstock, pp173: BlueOrange Studio/Shutterstock, pp175: MARTYN F. CHILLMAID/SCIENCE PHOTO LIBRARY, pp176: REVOR CLIFFORD PHOTOGRAPHY/SCIENCE PHOTO LIBRARY, pp176: Bart_J/Shutterstock, pp177: PAUL WHITEHILL/SCIENCE PHOTO LIBRARY, pp180: Erhan Dayi/Shutterstock, pp181: Mevans/iStockphoto, pp181: Ffolas/Shutterstock, pp183: JoeGough/iStockphoto, pp186: RicAguiar/iStockphoto, pp186: Anirut Krisanakul/Shutterstock, pp188: Natalia Barsukova/Shutterstock, pp188: Kovnir Andrii/Shutterstock, pp189: Chesh/Alamy, pp190: Terry Moore / Stocktrek Images/Alamy, pp190: Dario Sabljak/Alamy, pp190: Romakoma/Shutterstock, pp191: Sciencephotos/Alamy, pp192: Warren Price Photography/Shutterstock, pp192: Celiafoto/Shutterstock, pp192: Sergiy Zavgorodny/Shutterstock, pp193: Jorg Hackemann/Shutterstock, pp194: DonNichols/iStockphoto, pp194: Pete Pahham/Shutterstock, pp194: Simon g/Shutterstock, pp195: POWER AND SYRED/Science Photo Library, pp196: ARENA Creative/Shutterstock, pp196: MidoSemsem/Shutterstock, pp197: Ivonne Wierink/Shutterstock, pp202: Yann Arthus-Bertrand/Getty Images, pp202: Littlewitchz223/Shutterstock, pp202: ETAJOE/Shutterstock, pp203: Clive Streeter/Getty Images, pp204: Mint Images/Frans Lanting/Getty Images, pp204: B.G. Thomson/Science Photo Library, pp204: Juhku/Shutterstock, pp204: Vilainecrevette/Shutterstock, pp204: Holbox/Shutterstock, pp205: Maria Stenzel/Getty Images, pp206: Radius Images/Alamy, pp206: Brent Winebrenner/Getty Images, pp206: ART WOLFE/SCIENCE PHOTO LIBRARY, pp206: Ssnowball/Shutterstock, pp206: Kushch Dmitry/Shutterstock, pp206: Leonardo Gonzalez/Shutterstock, pp208: Ros Drinkwater/Alamy, pp208: M Timothy O'Keefe/Getty Images, pp208: Christine Norton/Shutterstock, pp208: S.Z./Shutterstock, pp209: Ron Zmiri/Shutterstock, pp210: Afoto6267/Shutterstock, pp211: Hiroya Minakuchi/Getty Images, pp211: Kwanbenz/Shutterstock, pp212: Adam Hurley/EyeEm/Getty Images, pp212: Elena Elisseeva/Shutterstock, pp213: Flirt/P. Bauer/Corbis/Alamy, pp213: Bernhard Richter/iStockphoto, pp213: Javarman/Shutterstock, pp214: FRANS LANTING, MINT IMAGES / SCIENCE PHOTO LIBRARY, pp214: Studiotouch/Shutterstock, pp220: Jorg Hackemann/Shutterstock.